Contents

References

The edition used is Gallimard (collection 'Folio Plus', no. 1), with a study dossier appendix compiled by Michel Bigot and Bruno Vercier. Page references to this are given in bold type within plain brackets.

Within the text, the style (IV, 1338) denotes citations from the NRF Gallimard 'Bibliothèque de la Pléiade' edition of Giono's *Œuvres romanesques complètes* (6 vols., 1971-1983), under the general editorship of Robert Ricatte. *Le Hussard sur le toit* is in volume IV, and critical presentation, notes and variants are supplied by Pierre Citron. *Récits* refers to the Pléiade volume of *Récits et essais*, ed. Citron (1989).

In the footnote and bibliographical citations that follow, the place of publication for works written in English and French is not stated unless other than London and Paris, respectively.

My most grateful thanks are due to Dr. Russell Cousins, of the University of Birmingham, and Dr. Charles Forsdick, of the University of Glasgow, who enabled me to compile an accurate list of film credits.

Walter Redfern Reading, June 1997

Jean Giono

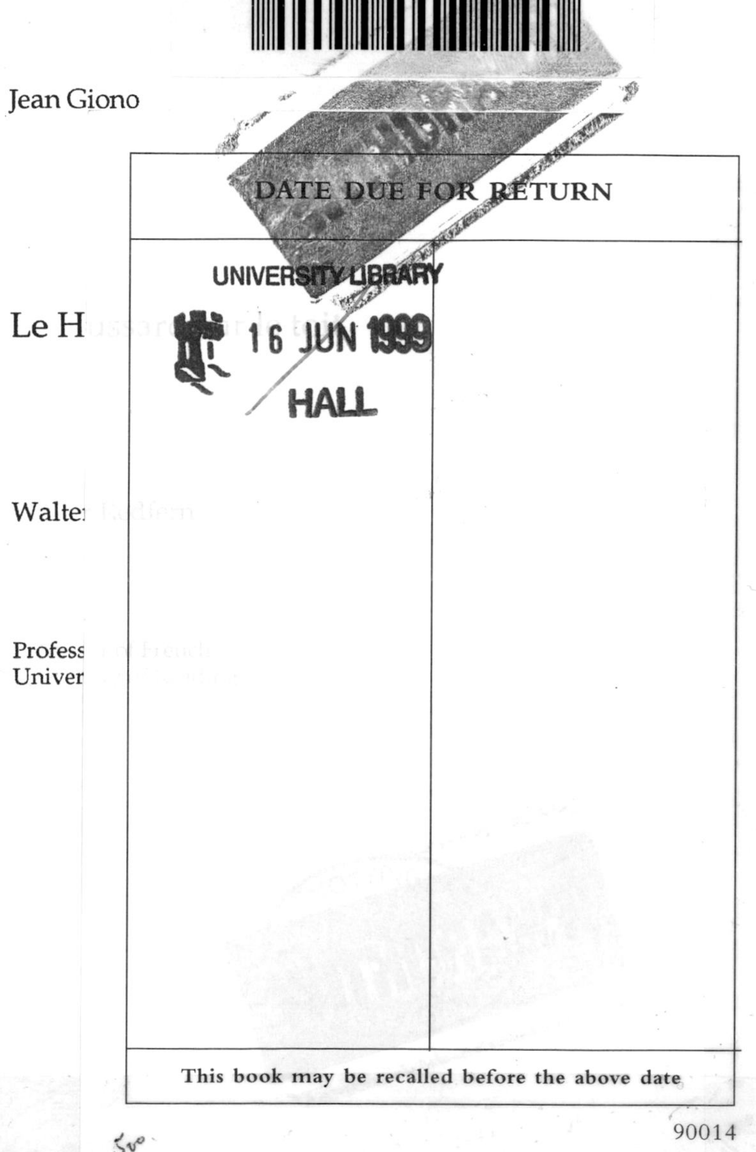

Le H

Walte

Profess
Univer

UNIVERSITY OF GLASGOW
FRENCH AND GERMAN PUBLICATIONS
1997

University of Glasgow French and German Publications

Modern Languages Building, University of Glasgow,
Glasgow G12 8QL, Scotland

First published 1997.

Printed by University of Glasgow Printing Department.

ISBN 0 85261 530 2

Overture

The career of Jean Giono (1895-1970) upsized from that of local bank-clerk to independent fabulist: uncreative accountancy gave way to galloping inflation. The pre-1939 novels which brought him widespread fame took off from his home base, 'Provence', and were never, despite critics' labels, regionalist in intention or practice. In the following decade, Giono more frankly talked of his 'Sud imaginaire' (comparable to William Faulkner's 'Yoknapatawpha County'—II, 1277). *Le Hussard sur le toit*, published in 1951, but started around 1945, is no more a historical novel than the preceding fictions were peasant novels.

In the 1930s, though a lifelong pacifist, Giono, in the face of growing dictatorships of Right or Left (Hitler, Stalin), dreamt vengefully of peasant Jacqueries which would destroy the modern industrialised world, and give birth not to a brave new one, but rather rebirth to older civilisations. In that period, his pen waxed increasingly apocalyptic. Unjustifiably imprisoned in 1939 for defeatist antimilitarism, and in 1944 for alleged collaboration during the war, Giono in fact harboured a Jew and Resistance workers on the run. He wrote an allegorical play, *Le Voyage en calèche*, whose hero was a dry run for Angelo Pardi in *Le Hussard sur le toit*. Julio commits himself to resistance against the French occupation of northern Italy in 1797. This play was banned by the German censors. Ironically, Giono the inveterate liar, who always had the greatest difficulty sticking to simple facts, was traduced, at the outset and termination of the war, by falsified interpretations of his activities on the part of those whom he called small-town Robespierres and partisans of the new *Terreur:* local Communists.[1]

Although they were published out of sequence, four texts by Giono relate to Angelo Pardi: *Angelo* (his two years in Aix); *Le Hussard sur le toit* (Angelo caught up with Pauline de Théus in

---

[1] On similar charges levelled against Marcel Aymé, that are reflected in his novel of the Occupation and its aftermath, see Christopher Lloyd, *Aymé: 'Uranus' / 'La Tête des autres'* (University of Glasgow French & German Publications, 1994), pp. 2-8.

a cholera epidemic); *Le Bonheur fou* (Angelo engaged in revolution in Italy); and *Mort d'un personnage* (the death of Pauline de Théus in old age, lovingly tended by the grandson of Angelo and herself). Giono caressed a project, typically never carried through, for a long series of at least ten novels, alternating between Angelo in the nineteenth century and his descendant in the twentieth. The plan was characteristically wild and woolly, shot through with inner contradictions. In the four published volumes, too, though Angelo has met Pauline already in *Angelo*, he meets her for the first time in *Le Hussard sur le toit*. The consummation of their love which produced the son must take place in some nether region, for they part chastely in this novel and do not meet again in *Le Bonheur fou*.

Giono falsely claimed that the genesis of Angelo dated back to the early 1930s, no doubt as an attempt to abolish the distinction many critics drew between his 'two manners', pre- and post-1939: timeless rural fictions and nineteenth-century chronicles. It is true, nonetheless, that Angelo is a (somewhat distant) cousin to the heroes of the earlier fictions, in his readiness to give of himself and to open up to the natural world. A recurrent figure in the prewar novels is 'le guérisseur', a man who has the power of healing and rescuing ill-used fellow-beings. This figure derives from Giono's partly mythified father, whom he called a 'condottiere assis': a stay-at-home adventurer (IV, 1123). As with Michel Tournier, the oxymoron 'le voyageur immobile' always enchanted Giono's imagination. Jean-Baptiste Giono, the father's father, was also turned into a legendary figure, credited unverifiably with being a Piedmontese *carbonaro*, and with nursing cholera victims in the Algeria of the 1830s. Literary models for Angelo included Stendhal's Julien Sorel and Fabrice del Dongo. This largely self-taught writer was thoroughly bookish.

Similarly he was not a peasant; he was an anti-townee. Sartre once likened him belittlingly to a small-town savant, 'un notaire qui rêve devant une carte.'[2] Indeed, Giono's folksy philosophising can often sound worthy of a cracker-barrel pundit in the archetypal *Café du Commerce*. Giono was not, however, untutored or naive. He was wily and widely read.

[2] J.-P. Sartre, in *Les Écrits de Sartre*. eds. M. Contat and M. Rybalka (Gallimard, 1970), p. 634.

Many, especially French critics, unable to square his undeniable imaginative powers with his structural shortcomings—a problem more than one reader has had with other rhapsodic writers such as Rabelais or Diderot—have foisted scaffoldings on his work, or even false beams. If challenged as to whether these imports are forcibly imposed, they take refuge in what must have been the extremely capacious unconscious of Giono. This apparently most literally down-to-earth of French writers has attracted, willy-nilly, heavily cerebral approaches. Yet, palpably, he thinks in images, hence the approximations, the wildness, but also the suggestiveness. All the same, he does not lack self-control, and is only as terrified as he wants to be. His supposed 'metaphysics' are more akin to reverie. Seated at his writing-desk, he imagines the worst, and best. He is not at ease in the median. Some atheists frighten themselves with hellfire; some incurable optimists entertain the prospect of disaster. What is Giono, the novelist of will and strength and healthiness, doing in, and with, a cholera epidemic? While never thinking seriously against himself, Giono obviously needs contrast, opposition, for the sake of renewal, as well as for the reaffirmation of what he holds dear. And. of course, in instigating chaos, the self-celebratory creator is still in charge, the lord of the *danse macabre.* The very title of this novel places a horseman, unusually, on a roof. In *Le Hussard sur le toit*, Giono is both holding his horses (especially as regards his hero's love-life), and giving them free rei(g)n.

Chapter One

Cholera and its adversaries

Giono adopted Stendhal's practice of 'la scène probante'—a dramatic situation which tests revealingly the moral fibre, the generosity of imagination, and the capacity for energetic deployment of will-power of a heroic protagonist—and extended it to a whole, long novel. The cholera epidemic tests the hero Angelo Pardi to the utmost. It represents the facts (and the fictions) of life that further his existential education.

Throughout recorded history, plagues have infected witnesses or fabulists with the desire to describe them, and, most often, to exploit the symbolic potential of these terrifying natural phenomena. The Greek historian Thucydides evoked plague in his account of the Peloponnesian War, Lucretius in his *De rerum natura*, Daniel Defoe in his *Journal of the Plague Year*, Thomas Mann in *Death in Venice*, and Camus in *La Peste*. Giono takes off, as on a trampoline, from this lengthy tradition. Besides, to shift to a metaphorical level, in his own previous work he had revelled in an epidemic of lying and image-making in *Naissance de l'Odyssée*, his version of how Ulysses's fabulous adventures were engendered. His 'Prélude de Pan' built up a monstrous vision of humans and beasts coupling, an apocalyptic punishment for human cruelty towards animals. Apocalyptic on a wider scale is the dam-burst, flooding whole valleys, in *Batailles dans la montagne*. In *Le Bonheur fou*, the man-made epidemic is revolution and war. The dominant pagan deity inhabiting Giono's work is the Great God Pan. Pan begets panic, pandemics. Plagues of all kinds afford Giono scope for his innate tendency to *démesure:* exorbitance.

His attitude to historical, geographical or scientific accuracy was bound to be cavalier. As the elder Dumas allegedly exclaimed in typically macho fashion: 'J'ai violé l'Histoire mais je lui ai fait des enfants' (cited IV, 1158). In *Le Hussard sur le toit*, Giono mixes up real and invented place names, so that any pious attempt at literary pilgrimage would fail. Just as in the opening scenes he uses the narratorial device of simultaneism, in order to capture the advance of the epidemic on several fronts at once, so he exploits the extensive documentation he collected on cholera in a way which ignores the revising and updating of scientific discovery. It is not scientific accuracy that interests him, but the spread, the variety, of opinions on the phenomenon, false or true: the human compulsion to have your say. Curiosity and invention matter far more to him than fidelity to observed fact. Citron, after cross-checking with Giono's library on cholera, notes, to give one example, that the most insistent simile of the whole text, vomit likened to 'riz au lait' (milky rice pudding), figures in none of the medical treatises. Citron concludes that Giono creates his own version of the epidemic (IV, 1357). For instance, Giono suggests that the cholera was introduced into Provence by the frigate *Melpomène* (the muse of tragedy—perhaps the lovely name appealed to him), whereas in fact this ship was successfully used as a place of quarantine in Toulon.[3] Giono conflates accounts of bubonic plagues (e.g. that of 1720) with cholera outbreaks. In 1838, the year of this novel's action, cholera was not significantly active (it was in 1834). Blithely, Giono slips in anachronisms: the railway said to operate in the Rhône Valley in 1838 was not in service till 1855. He exaggerates the death rate (but gods, including writers, those little gods, enjoy powers of life and death over populations). Like Siva, Giono executes, more than the epidemic did. But also like Siva, he gives life, even to death.

His epidemic, like any real-life one, instals chaos, *la chienlit* (from 'chie-en-lit', which is what its victims uncontrollably do).

[3] As further evidence of the tendency of Giono and / or folk mythology to conflate this into 'Miasmes délétères à bord de la *Melpomène*' (**34**; **39**), we may consider the following, strictly contemporary, account. A doctor who treated the 1835 epidemic in Toulon wrote of how: three ships, including the *Melpomène*, were forced to observe a period of quarantine by anchoring at the island in the roads where stood a lazaret dedicated to the patron of plagues, Saint Roch; thanks to this precautionary isolation, the disease did not reach the mainland, which may not have been so when, if it still bore the 'choléra de Lisbonne', the *Melpomène* tied up in the harbour of Marseille; another ship, the *Amériquaine*, was quarantined because it carried 'celui de l'Inde', more clearly Asiatic in origin (Hubert Lauvergne, *Choléra-morbus en Provence* [Toulon: A. Aurel, 1836], pp. 1-2). Although the work is not to be found in the list of medical sources known to have been consulted by Giono (IV, 1308-1309), these three facets of a possible origin of the epidemic are amalgamated in the first chapter; see also the version given in 'Cent Mille Morts' (IV, 1472). [Editor's note].

This word is also inexplicably connected with carnival masks. Carnival is a different form of havoc, the world turned upside down. People often don masks to ward off plagues. A man encountered by Angelo and Pauline informs them of the festive atmosphere in some towns hit by the epidemic:

> Nous sommes en plein moyen âge, monsieur. On brûle à tous les carrefours des épouvantails bourrés de paille qu'on appelle 'le père choléra'; on l'insulte, on se moque de lui. (**338**)

Giono alludes to *opera buffa*, and to Punch and Judy:

> Le volet d'une des maisons de la place s'ouvrit avec fracas et parut le buste d'un homme et des bras qui gesticulaient. [...] il virevoltait dans le cadre de sa fenêtre ouverte comme un guignol sur sa scène. (**164**)

Many of the descriptions of dying or dead bodies underline their semblance of wearing heavy make-up. Some victims lie indecently displaying their genitals, shameless about their pudenda, in a kind of terminal striptease. All of this is the *spectacle* of death, 'le théâtre de sang' (VI, 95-6), also sponsored by writers such as Sade, Artaud and Genet. The casualties are violently agitated, often mechanically like puppets, but also at times dynamically, as if dying involved passion and energy; as if they are dead but they won't lie down. Even the gaping mouth of a corpse can retain a shocking vestige of life: an obscenely pink tongue betokening human voracity and desire. People die twitching, grimacing, writhing, literally biting the dust. They die furious, ravenous, as in the idiom 'manger les pissenlits par la racine'. Angelo's attempts at behavioural sang-froid, his preference for what the abbé Sieyès is said to have termed 'la mort sans phrases', contrasts with the desperate histrionics of the moribund.

Death is no respecter of persons, so in response why not countervail it, however unavailingly, with irreverence, as in the sardonic adverbs, the far from morose delectation, in this passage:

> Un spectacle *heureusement* très insolent. C'étaient trois cadavres dans lesquels le chien et les oiseaux avaient fait beaucoup de dégâts. *Notamment* dans un enfant de quelques

> mois écrasé sur la table comme un gros fromage blanc. Les deux autres, *vraisemblablement* celui d'une vieille femme et celui d'un homme assez jeune étaient ridicules avec leurs têtes de pitres fardées de bleu, leurs membres désarticulés, leurs ventres bouillonnants de boyaux et de vêtements hachés et pétris. (**50-51**; my emphasis)

This scene recalls one in *Le Grand Troupeau* (1931), in which Giono relived the carnage of the Great War: crows feasting off soldiers' corpses. Some readers might feel that in such descriptions Giono aestheticises death, as in this phrase: 'C'est le plus beau débarquement de choléra asiatique qu'on ait jamais vu' (**57**). 'Beau', however, is here antiphrastic, as in many idioms ('un beau salaud', 'nous voilà dans de beaux draps'). The refrain of the sickly-sweet smell of death embodies the mixture of nausea and attraction felt by onlookers, those temporary survivors. It is often maintained that death in the twentieth century is the one remaining taboo. We shut it away in hospices; even in hospitals the screens go round the deathbed. Death used to be a more public event. In *Le Hussard sur le toit*, it forcibly becomes so: people die on the streets. The special horror of epidemics, of course, is that corpses themslves are dangerous: they secrete the lethal germs after as well as before death. They are infectious, too, in that they act as a model for copycat behaviour: 'les vivants reproduisaient, par une sorte de singerie luciférienne, les convulsions d'agonie dont ils avaient eu le spectacle' (**193**). For both insiders and bystanders, death mesmerises. As it offers a jump into the unknown, the void, it induces vertigo.

In this novel, death often appears unreal because it is excessively real, hyperreal; it is too much for human minds, and of course bodies, to cope with: it is *la démesure* itself. While Giono always belittled the wrong use of *démesure*: the vaunted exploits of the machine age and mass civilisation, the obsession with the amassing of material goods, the spiralling control of private lives by bureaucratic governments, he equally always championed the right use: in the imagination, passions, individualism. In *Le Hussard sur le toit*, he recycles the binary patterns of the earlier *Noé* (1947): *avarice* and *perte*. In the novel, the cholera forces people to curl up foetally, centripetally (*avarice*), but also to splay themselves centrifugally (*perte*). The cholera itself passes through different stages and manifestations: it can be, at one time, e.g. 'foudroyant' (poleaxing). At one time, its action is compared to a sniper picking off sitting ducks; at another, it is the king of beasts: 'Maintenant, le choléra marchait comme un lion à travers villes et bois' (**289**). In *Noé*, four years earlier, Giono described 'le choléra ou la peste' as 'des dieux en chair et en os' (III, 771). An epidemic, for Giono, could never be a simple social, historical, medical phenomenon. The gods are amongst us, as in Homer, in archaic or tribal societies, and in our twentieth-century versions of these. This plague is high in the cast list, a dramatic protagonist in its own right. One of the major literary themes has always been Man versus It (the ocean, jungle, mountains, animal invasion). Like a god (e.g. Pan), the cholera here gets everywhere, seems unstoppable, has a mysterious will of its own, and sets up its own systems of cause and effect, and of arbitrary punishment.

Before studying the hero Angelo and his confrontation with this alien power, we need to examine its catastrophic impact on society generally. Firstly, countermeasures. Giono provides hardly any doctors, nurses, or properly organised hospitals, though he does feature rough quarantines. Herding people into insanitary quarantines simply multiplies the infections. The sanctuary mutates into a knacker's yard. When Angelo notices that, despite accelerating fatalities, bourgeois refugees feel safer in quarantines, he mutters *'Continua la commedia'* (**380**). Apart from a prayer service briefly glimpsed, a religious procession in a largely deserted town, and the activities of a few nuns, the input of the Catholic Church is reduced virtually to zero. Despite emphasising the presence of (largely inoperative) barricades, Giono clearly wanted as few blockers or intermediaries as possible between the disease and the diseased. The army has a certain role, but it is largely ineffective. Ignorance is rife. Melons or tomatoes are variously blamed for the contagion; food, which sustains life, is here held to bring death. Remedies such as paregoric elixir, a mixture of camphor and opium, imbibed on a sugar lump, prove futile. A doctor met by Angelo asserts that the only effective remedies 'contre cette saloperie-là' are the two old, last-ditch ones: 'la flamme ou la fuite' (**58**). Accordingly, infected corpses are burnt on mass funeral pyres. In the text 'Cent Mille Morts', on which the short film *Le Foulard de Smyrne* was based, it is written:

> ... il n'y a de ressource qu'en Dieu.
> Ou dans le feu qui est un dieu primitif, un destructeur de matières plus efficace. (IV, 1472)

In the absence of remedies to ward off the cholera (the available ones are as useless as rotten bargepoles), people have *attitudes*. Giono enjoys himself, uncensorially, with relating the primitive superstitions bred by disasters. We hear yarns of a dog giving responses in a catechism class (**359**); of the spontaneous combustion of corpses (**248**); of horse-shaped comets (**152**). The latter image obviously resurrects the Four Horsemen of the Apocalypse. Rural myths add to urban ones. One person gives a very detailed account of a flock of military crows, disciplined, on parade, and commanded by a hidden voice (**360**). Such fallacies do little active harm, unlike more brutal forms of response. A mob, largely composed of women, lynches a man suspected wrongly of polluting water supplies; it is described as a murderous gang rape: 'Elles rugissaient une sorte de grondement sourd qui venait de la gorge et avait beaucoup de rapport avec la volupté' (**143**), as they kick in the supine man's head with their heels. One of these stays lodged and the woman keels over, unbalanced. When several of the lynchers then begin to topple like ninepins, struck by the cholera, Angelo briefly gloats at this savage poetic justice (**144**).

In the chaos of the epidemic, it is every woman and man for himself and herself. Movement is stampede. Like voyeurs at crash scenes, survivors gape ghoulishly at the dying. Public order breaks down into looting. As Citron comments, 'la peur est comme un second choléra, presque aussi meurtrier' (IV, 1359). Fear, of course, is a necessary biological reflex in the face of rampant death, but fear in this novel takes the cruellest, most egoistic forms. Humans produce waste, and here are waste, to be put out at night-time, unceremoniously disposed of. Provence becomes one vast death camp.

Angelo

In *Le Hussard sur le toit*, Angelo Pardi feels more truly alive when dangerously tending cholera victims than when, in *Le Bonheur fou*, he fights in order to discern which side in the

Italian war of so-called liberation is the least unidealistic. Involvement and expenditure of self are also, in his eyes, better than simply existing, safer though this be: 'Il voyait ici un pays sans choléra ni révolution mais il le trouvait triste' (**352**). His partly egotistic, partly altruistic, pursuit of happiness distinguishes him from the mainly unhappy egoism of most of his fellows.

As a character, Angelo is designed as streamlined in order to give him less wind resistance on his often headlong rides across Provence, and to enable him to eel out of tricky fixes. He possesses lissom muscular grace, but also sensitivity. He appeals to women of all ages and social conditions. He is a greenhorn, and has to learn the ropes of the desperate situation in which he is embroiled. On the first page, he starts open-mouthed, at dawn (later, corpses' mouths are gaping holes). His naivety and his capacity for surprise and wonderment are instantly and durably captured. Like Stendhal's Fabrice del Dongo, he relies on imported models to boost his native qualities: 'English' composure to add to his inborn 'Italian' brio: 'il était assez content de son air froid qu'il imaginait très anglais' (**299**). Yet he re-energises these stereotypes, just as Giono sharpens the teeth of old saws ('ne pas chercher midi à quatorze heures'; 'ne pas mettre les bouchées doubles'). On many occasions Angelo is curt. He refuses to make a song and dance about the catastrophe, which is itself hyperbolically gasbag. His self-esteem is every bit as important to him as the respect he might win from others. His journeys are initiatory, and these initiations come from both people and non-human sources: crows, pigs, trees, landscapes, the cholera itself. His encounters with the disease help to define him, to himself as well as to others; it is a learning experience. For our part, inasmuch as we readers are filled in about Angelo, it is only gradually as the narrative progresses. Angelo warns his foster brother Giuseppe, and Giono warns the pigeonholing reader: 'N'oublie pas que je bouge, [...] et que je ne poserai jamais pour le portrait' (**268**). The epigraph to the novel comes from the Spanish Golden Age playwright Calderón, but, like so many of Giono's sources, it is adapted for his own purposes. Condemned by the Inquisition, the Calderón character is burnt in effigy (*estatua*). Angelo's 'statue' is his own self-image which he pursues.

Giono familiarises us with Angelo's accoutrements, which are an intimate part of him. Firstly, his sword: he killed Baron Swartz, the Austrian spy, with one, an act which necessitated Angelo's flight to France; and he will likewise kill Giuseppe in *Le Bonheur fou.* In *Le Hussard sur le toit*, his sword and his dexterity with it rescue him from several parlous situations. He disarms professional soldiers with almost ridiculous ease, even when he is equipped with a paltry specimen, 'un coupe-chou' (**72**). He brandishes his pistols, but he is just as adept at fisticuffs and putting the boot in. He has a string of horses, on whose back he is happier than anywhere else. On horseback, above all, he enacts the difference between the quick and the dead. He smokes small cigars, a sign of his aristocratic elegance, as are his exquisite boots; if he has to die, let it be shod in these. Earlier he was an officer in the army of the King of Sardinia, but his adoring mother had bought his colonel's commission. Everybody recognises his breeding, and several comment on it, sometimes derisively, but he himself, as a bastard, believes he has to win his spurs and his 'titres de noblesse'.

Giono tells us of, but also shows in action, Angelo's 'impérieux besoin de générosité' (**107**), a term which embraces Cornelian heroics, idealistic romanticism, and humanitarian service. He ingenuously swears, at one moment, that he could prove to fearful people that 'la générosité est plus terrible que le choléra' (**88**). His impetuosity leaves him open to being duped, which he detests above all. Despite the image with which Giono signalled Angelo's arrival as a vision in his study (in *Noé,* but repeated in *Le Hussard sur le toit*)—'un épi d'or sur son cheval noir' (**137**)—Angelo was no product of virgin birth. His genitors include Ariosto, Cervantes, and Stendhal. His name might suggest 'angel', but Giono makes little play with this possibility, except to evoke 'le ravissement le plus angélique' (**294**) when his hero gets away from quarantine on his horse. Though a splendid human being, Angelo is no angel, nor is he the envoy of some superior power, unless it be the author himself.He has had a before, and will have an after, as well as the intense now of this novel. Periodically Giono ensures that Angelo looks dishevelled, filthy, ludicrous, something other than a golden ear of corn. Is he a knight 'sans peur et sans reproche'? He often panics, quakes in his boots, even if he does not beshit himself. He is remarkably free from any desire to manipulate or exploit others. He is ever ready to serve, while declaring, in good anarchist fashion '*Non serviam!*' Attitude is the bottom line, the name of the game. If you have the right attitude (etymologically linked to 'aptitude'), you are fit to tackle anything. Angelo is a hero with attitude—quick to respond, not to be trifled with, lastingly concerned with posture—whether it is in fencing, in the saddle, or in moral stances. Giono talks of 'cette négligence toujours instinctivement calculée' (**139**). Angelo justifies this oxymoron, by rehearsing spontaneity, 'préparant une petite phrase très désinvolte' (**55**). He is twenty-five years old, yet he is often addressed and treated as though he were a child or youth, presumably because those he meets sense the vulnerability beneath the tough exterior, 'cet air sec et détaché qui était la défense habituelle de sa timidité' (**13**).

While pregnable to the opinion or hostility of others, he is also his own harshest critic:

> Tu ne pourras jamais, ne disons pas agir mais seulement parler comme tout le monde [...]. N'emploieras-tu jamais les mots café au lait et pantoufles? (**237**)

In fact, he readily talks of such common-or-garden things. That self-accusation leads on to a reflexion on the heroism of everyday life—one of Giono's oldest and sturdiest hobbyhorses—it is ordinary people who make history merely by getting on with the business of life and love (*ibid.*). Angelo knows he is an exaggerator; his eye is as it were faceted, like a fly's, and therefore aggrandising:

> Mes yeux ne regardent qu'à travers les loupes [...] je ne suis pas simple: je suis double, triple, et même centuple. (**236**)

This delineation is clearly itself hyperbolic. More prosaically, to counteract his stomach cramps, possibly a signal of infection, his remedy is to concoct and quaff a powerful red wine punch and a home-made loaf: bread and wine, here not a sacrament but a prophylactic. He vomits several times, a different kind of outpouring from what Giono called his 'générosité immense, hémorrhagique' (IV, 1122). To buck himself up, he often curses himself: 'Foutue poule mouillée [...]. Il se parlait en langage sergent pour se donner du cœur au ventre' (**52**): he is his own sergeant-major. Language, too, can thus be a health precaution. But it can also have little or no effect. In one section, after roundly telling himself off (always a paradoxical act, as if the ego could split in two), he ends up as before, 'prêt à toutes les folies' (**238**).

In the long section on the roofs of Manosque, which gives the novel its title, is Angelo, like the pacifist Romain Rolland, 'au-dessus de la mêlée'? Giono clearly exploits here that 'élévation' (of position, of character) that appealed to both Stendhal and the Camus of *L'Étranger*. Roofs are the opposite of jails, and prisoners take to them in protest. This sanctuary, however, only remains such if Angelo stays up there on the tiles, so that it is in effect an open-air prison. All the same, it affords a breathing space after all his careering gallops or daylong plods: time for meditation, moral accountancy. It is also the turning point, for in this period he first meets Pauline, who will subsequently give far more meaningful focus to his previously rather random errantry. The roofs are, and foreshadow, a whole new world, which is frequently likened to a stalled ocean:

> De courtes vagues immobiles d'une extraordinaire rigueur couvraient d'un ressac anguleux et glacé l'emplacement de la ville. (**135**)

This is the paradox of a mobile still life. The rooftops are thus not a stable milieu, even though Angelo gradually learns to feel confidently at home on the sloping tiles and pinnacles. At times he experiences vertigo:

> Des cours intérieures, noires et attirantes comme des gueules de puits. [...] Ces profondeurs aspiraient. (**146**)

Like Pauline later harassed by an insistent crow, he briefly experiences the downward pull to death, the seductiveness of dying. He too is attacked by flocks of birds—swallows, in a counter-cliché, for these are never usually thought of as threatening. When glimpsed by citizens below, the largely sinless Angelo is superstitiously taken for the Devil (**167**). He has, however, his inner demons. After the swallow attack, he falls asleep and dreams of being smothered beneath a vast cockerel, scrabbling to break free and grabbing only handfuls of guano in the shape of a little girl's face (**161-2**)—the child he had watched earlier parading with obscenely blithe normalcy through the vacated streets of the town (**156-7**). Closing the eyes is dangerous, a possible trapdoor to the big sleep of death; vigilance is crucial.

When he descends to street level, where previously he had been all but lynched on suspicion of poisoning a public fountain, Angelo is taught more lessons by the rotund nun he meets: 'Elle était ronde comme une barrique. Deux griffes de petites moustaches noires agrafaient sa bouche de chaque côté' (**187**).[4] Angelo is 'littéralement séduit' (**199**). She speaks to him mainly in the imperative mood, to which the good soldier in him responds well: she is, after all, a superior mother. She sweetens her caustic tongue with periodic snippets of tenderness: 'Mon petit!' (**189**). Her speech is performative: she weds the action to the word. She teaches by example the supreme virtue of elbow-grease: 'Du jus de coude!' (*ibid.*). Washing corpses is a simple, necessary job well done. She is 'tout d'une pièce' (*ibid.*); she has 'une étonnante présence' (**190**). Her own stoical attitude to death is one she wishes to transmit to the dying:

> «Allons, allons! dit-elle, un peu de patience. Tout le monde y arrive; ça va venir. On y est, on y est. Ne te force pas, ça vient tout seul. Doucement, doucement. Chaque chose en son temps.» (**189**)

The cholera is frenzy; she is serenity. 'Où elle était, tout s'ordonnait. Elle entrait et les murs ne contenaient plus de drames' (**190**). Where Angelo is tempted to *démesure*, the nun is all *mesure*, limited objectives. Her example offsets that of the materialistic, exploitative nuns who are later found in charge of a quarantine (**370**).

In the text 'Recherche de la pureté', Giono wrote of the angelic longing to rid his body and whole being of the filthy carnage he had to live through at the Front in the 1914-1918 War (*Récits*, 635-56). From his own experience of two imprisonments, he has Angelo, trapped in a quarantine, reflect:

---

[4] The sexual and other magnetism of fat women surfaces in other Giono texts, e.g. *Ennemonde*.

> Ce ne sont pas les fers ni les murs qui gardent les prisonniers en prison: c'est l'odeur de leurs latrines qu'ils sont obligés de renifler pendant des mois, puis des années. Avec des sens avilis, quel monde voulez-vous qu'ils aient en eux? (**389**)

In *Le Hussard sur le toit*, he plunges his largely pure young man into such filth, dirties his hands by putting him under the thumb of the nun. Her faith is straightforward: she wants corpses clean for the Resurrection. She is not a nurse but a charlady of bodies: 'J'approprie [...] . Le jour de la résurrection ils seront propres' (**197**). Appropriately, the narrative waxes biblical around her: Moses, curses, the ire of God (**191**). Smoking his cigars, she teaches Angelo the value of doggedness. Hers is a simple goodness: rightness, not righteousness. Angelo knows very well that their conjoined efforts, their Augean labours, are perfectly useless, cosmetic; but 'la passion pour l'inutile' energised a whole community in *Que ma joie demeure* (II, 438). Angelo, who loathes the posturing he occasionally succumbs to, can in this episode reassure himself that he is posing for no audience (**203**). We should note the *distinguo:* 'Il avait le goût de la supériorité et la terreur de l'affectation' (*ibid.*). Accurately, he reminds himself: 'C'est à toi qu'il ne faut pas céder' (**205**). Immersing yourself in filth is not to be sniffed at, nor taken with deathly seriousness. When one night a corpse sits up, the nun is offended: 'Tu m'as trompée' (**208**). Summoned by her order, she disappears from Angelo's view. Both she and Angelo survive their perilous proximity to the disease. In Camus's *La Peste,* Dr Rieux cites the story of a Persian town where an epidemic killed everyone except the corpse-washer who carried on throughout.

The cholera does not inspire uniform behaviour. Angelo's encounters with other people embrace commercial interchange, dangerous confrontation, altruism (on both sides), ignoble conduct (Angelo learns to cope with 'la canaillerie à deux pieds' [77] as well as with the cholera), and love. At times, Giono lets rip his disgust at how low some can sink:

> L'homme avait un visage d'une grossièreté stupéfiante et sur lequel on aurait dit qu'on avait à plaisir collectionné les stigmates les plus bas et les plus dégoûtants. (**75**)

On the other hand, Angelo can savour even blatant egoism; he is fascinated by one man's perfected version (**76**). There are, of course, mediocrities, unexceptional humanity. But Giono prefers to dwell on those who stand out, provocatively, who risk everything. A key example of an exception to the general rule of self first is the hard-working, ironic-eyed young doctor who teaches Angelo by example the saving grace of humour, and the absolute imperative of trying to salvage every remnant of life in any nook. It is he who names the disease: 'le choléra *morbus*' (**56**). Working alongside him in exhausting and always unsuccessful attempts to stop victims dying, Angelo falls into the robotic rhythms of 'frictionnement': rubbing bodies vigorously, continuously, as if to massage them back into health. Such unstinting automatism cannot defeat the mechanics of the disease. Wrestling with a flailing patient, Angelo feels 'la détente irrésistible d'un ressort d'acier' (**114**). Why do the pair go on trying? It seems to be beside the point to talk of the egoism of altruism. It is more of a Promethean stoicism, a refusal to let negation go uncontested: 'Il suffisait de quelques gestes très simples' (**193**). This agenda links the doctor and the nun in practice, though their teleology differs. The doctor will remain a vital model for Angelo in the rest of the story: '«Voilà comment il faut être!»' (**57**).

Others encountered are simply idiosyncratic. In Manosque, Angelo comes across a draper who absurdly keeps his shop open in a deserted town, and in his own daft way gainsays the cholera: 'Choléra, c'est beaucoup dire et c'est avec des mots qu'on fait peur' (**212**). Angelo recognises that maybe this man is right: 'Le mensonge est une vertu' (*ibid.*), one of Giono's most deeply-rooted beliefs, the efficacy of bloody-mindedness.

Angelo's biological mother, unlike most progenitors, fears that her son will *not* do crazy things. Her long letter to him is a praise of folly: 'Tu peux être grave et fou, qui empêche?' (**256**), for she knows his concern for stylishness, which she has instilled. 'Sois toujours imprudent, mon petit, c'est la seule façon d'avoir un peu de plaisir dans notre époque de manufactures' (**235**). She tells him of the metaphorical plague in Turin: rabid politics. Only sixteen years older than her son, she talks to him in the tones of a high-minded, incestuous passion reminiscent of Gina's for Fabrice in *La Chartreuse de Parme*. She breathes a kind of attitudinal racism. Of Angelo's duel with Baron Swartz, she comments on the fact that the clean kill bears a family signature, as recognized by a police superintendent:

> L'embêtant c'est que vous signez vos coups [...] ils ont tous dix ans de pratique et trois cents ans de désinvolture héréditaire. (**258**)

She boasts of her own ludic politicking, her manipulation of lesser mortals, which she could do in her sleep (**259**). People who take themselves seriously 'se font une vie dangereusement constipée' (**256**). She talks of Angelo and Giuseppe as Romulus and Remus, with Theresa as their lupine wet-nurse (**257**). When she says of the voracious Theresa: 'Elle voudrait être tout' and that she is madly jealous of Giuseppe's woman, Lavinia, she is also speaking for her own unbridled, possessive passion for Angelo. If she had known of it, this mother would have been insanely jealous of her son's relationship with Pauline de Théus.

Pauline

Pauline is prefigured in the bodies of three attractive young women, one of whom Angelo vainly tries to save, as he will indeed save Pauline. It is as if the wandering hero were being led towards Pauline: their chance encounter will prove to be inevitable. In fact, Pauline appears briefly, in the opening panorama, many miles away from Angelo, and experiencing the effects of the cholera for the first time when her servant dies on an errand (**25**). Before their first actual meeting in Manosque, prowling around roofs and cock-lofts, Angelo comes upon an attic storing clothes and footwear: 'Une odeur de [...] cœurs tendres, de jeunesse imputrescible, de passions bleues et de tisane de violette venait du beau grenier' (**172**). His response is a non-specific fetishism. He recalls (from *Angelo*) Anna Clèves saying to him: 'Heureusement que tu n'aimes pas l'amour', and thinks to himself:

> Serais-tu timide, par hasard? Il faut convenir que j'adore ces vêtements pendus aux murs. là-bas. [...] il humait l'odeur d'âmes qu'il imaginait sublimes. (**173-4**)

Clearly, a kind of metonymic displacement is operating here: not the part for the whole, but the accessory, the clothing, for the person. Yet it is a complete world that he summons up, of which this small space is the microcosm:

> .... je suis capable de créer un être qui chausse ces souliers, revêt ces robes, [...] et marche dans ce grenier (qui est d'ailleurs un parc, un château, un domaine, un pays avec son parlement)... (**174-5**)

So the fetishism entails imagination, empathy, love in advance. This scene prepares for the entrancing entrance of this visualised 'être', Pauline, whose body, of course, will be moulded by her own clothes.

In a dark house where Angelo is padding about in search of food and drink, he suddenly sees her:

> Elle tenait un chandelier à trois branches à la hauteur d'un petit visage en fer de lance encadré de lourds cheveux bruns. (**177**)

This lanceolate face is her leitmotif, her trademark. It suggests both the delicacy of flowers and the steel core and uprightness of a personality. The whole of her is seductive, without her making any effort to appear so. Predictably, Angelo feels bashful, gauche, and can say only: «Je suis un gentilhomme» (**178**). Pauline is totally unfazed by the intrusion of this unkempt and dirty young man in her house. After a few words, she acts decisively: 'Nos bagatelles de la porte sont ridicules' (**179**). This is on her part (and who knows on Giono's?) an inadvertent pun. 'Bagatelles de la porte': keeping someone chatting on the doorstep, but also a barker's come-on spiel outside a fairground booth, and sexual foreplay. The first sense is factual; the second ill suits her natural elegance; but the third prepares for a long-term coming event. For the moment, terribly English, she prepares for the dehydrated and famished Angelo vast bowls of tea and chunks of wholesome bread to dunk in it. For once, Angelo's recurrent self-criticism relents: «Je suis bête comme chou. [...] Au moins l'es-tu d'une façon naturelle?» (**181**).

Events then separate them for a considerable span of the text. When they meet again by providential chance at a barricade which thwarts their separate progress, they do not at first recognise each other. Angelo had earlier registered her beauty, her calm courage, her total lack of unnecessary fuss, but, as they travel on together, they get to know each other more thoroughly, and the sharing of dangers strongly unites them. Throughout, we see her actions, hear her words, but otherwise our view of her is essentially that of Angelo. We are never made privy, as with him, to her inner thoughts or feelings. The facts of her previous life are only very gradually vouchsafed to us as to Angelo. She is married to a much older man, a legitimist, who is still, at sixty-eight, a daredevil. She is an excellent rider, and handles pistols confidently. When tested, she is brave as an (exceptional) man. Like Angelo she abominates barricades, frontiers, quarantines, and feels an equal disgust for ignobly accidental death. She calmly claims: 'L'audace est mon giron naturel' (**443**).

For his part, Angelo's protective instincts towards her are at times military: 'Il pensait à la jeune femme comme à des chariots d'arrière-garde qu'il faut protéger à tout prix' (**311**). In a deserted house, he sleeps across her doorway like a guard-dog (**455**). He shows loving concern for her body (he briefly acknowledges she has lovely legs), by insisting on her wearing woollen stockings to keep her feet toast-warm as a basis for resisting illness. When he suggests, with a blush, that her riding style, astride, might have grazed her thighs, she reassures him by saying that she has ridden horses since childhood in this fashion, and always wears leather breeches under her skirt (**335**). Before her, Angelo is often tongue-tied and apologetic.

Alone for some moments at an overnight camp, Pauline is picked on by a carrion crow—the traditional harbinger, familiar or embodiment of death. She had fallen asleep, like Angelo on the roof before the swallow attack. The scene is forshadowed by a slightly earlier one, when Pauline and Angelo hear birds calling seductively, 'une sorte de tendresse persuasive, de force amoureuse qui tendait à contraindre, gentiment mais fermement' (**313**). Pauline calls these bird calls 'une cour pressante'. The crow is more shameless, sinister and violent, slashing at her sleeping eyes. She looses off a pistol shot at it. When Angelo rushes back to her on hearing the report, she tells him, with 'une horrible grimace de rire pendant que les larmes inondaient ses joues', that she felt 'sucrée [sickly-sweet] de la tête aux pieds et envie de fermer l'œil' (**317**). She confesses: 'Je comprenais tout et je me rendais compte que j'acceptais, que j'étais d'accord' (**318**). Rather than the old husband's tale that women secretly assent to rape, her response indicates that even the yea-saying Pauline feels the call to death. The laceration caused by the crow's beak just under her eye might be the source of her infection, for the crows have glutted themselves on cholera victims.

In quarantine, possibly because the cholera is already at work in her, Pauline seems at a low ebb, almost ready to emulate the unimaginative bourgeois ensconced there, and to surrender to death if she must (**388**). So near home and safety (she is making for her sister-in-law's château), she succumbs, vomits the horribly familiar milky fluid, and collapses.She is described as laughing like a beast of prey; it is almost the rictus of death (**489**). Having just been all but overwhelmed by the apocalyptic vision of the hermit-doctor (treated later), Angelo knows instantly that he is face to face with the mightiest foe he has ever encountered. As with the crow, Pauline is being summoned, with seductive violence. 'Angelo écouta ces appels étranges auxquels tout le corps de la jeune femme répondait' (**488**). Her response can be heard, and read, as sexual:

> Les gémissements de la jeune femme jaillissaient maintenant assez forts et sous le coup de spasmes. C'était une plainte continue [...], un paroxysme où le cri alors devenait sauvage et comme délirant. (**490**)

Amidst all the noisome filth pouring out of her body at both ends, Angelo soldiers on with the only antidote he knows: non-stop, vigorous massage. In one brief stop, he drinks from the same water bottle he has just put to her infected lips. Precautions have no place in this seemingly terminal and climactic coming together of their flesh. He has had to strip her up to her chest, a gesture she tries to resist with an icy hand: 'J'aime mieux mourir' (*ibid.*). But Angelo's 'fureur tendre' makes him denude her like skinning a rabbit. Sex is friction, the rubbing of two bodies together. In all this episode desire is not absent, though Angelo concentrates totally on the job in hand. Desire is an undercurrent, an electric charge. 'Zealous' and 'jealous' share roots (both covered by *jaloux* in French). Angelo's zeal to rescue Pauline is jealous: he fights for her against his arch-rival, Death. Love marries the centripetal *avarice* and the centrifugal *perte:* getting and spending. In later life, Giono's heart-condition obliged him to give up salt. He made a creative meal of this medical veto, just as his latter-day heroes and heroines find joy in not enjoying the normal fruits of consuming sexual happiness. Angelo sees Pauline at her physical best and worst, and he feels the same towards her. In *Mort d'un personnage*, the aged Pauline recalls her near-death from cholera. She lives for Angelo, through her memories of him. Their grandson tends her as selflessly in her terminal mess as her original lover did in *Le Hussard sur le toit*.

Giono attributed to William Faulkner this goal: 'Décrire tout, sauf l'objet, et il apparaît dans ce qui manque' (III, 1278). Desire can be conspicuous by its (apparent) absence. In this perspective, deletion, or hints, replace emphasis. In the troubadour tradition, 'amor de lonh' suggests both love *from* a distance and love *of* distance—that 'distance respectueuse' which becomes so obsessive a theme in Giono's later work. In *Pour saluer Melville*, the (fictional) love of Herman Melville and Adelina White is likewise, despite coincidence of desire, impossible. Though Angelo and Pauline never mention the end-stopped nature of their relationship and, mission accomplished, Angelo will move back to Italy and the revolution, they both know this imminent future is the inflexible parameter of their present. Their love is literally a metaphor: it is a bridge, a discovering of likeness in difference, an abolition of separateness.

The young couple and her husband have been compared to Tristram, Isolde and King Mark, though the analogy fits only awkwardly, for M. de Théus is the opposite of a coward and has no reason to doubt the loyalty of his young wife. Angelo's sense of honour rues out any avowal or display of love. Similarly his son, in *Mort d'un personnage*:

> ... reculait tout le temps devant l'amour de Caille [...], faisant de ses reculs les plus grandes preuves d'amour qu'un homme puisse donner. (*IV*, 187)

Such self-denial is undoubtedly noble if, for some tastes, frustrating. Whereas Giono indulges himself wantonly in his descriptions of flora, fauna or cholera, he stints us (and himself, gladly) in the area of physical love. Before the Second World War, this ostensibly most Lawrentian of all French writers was already expressing his distaste for putting sex on paper:

> Le gouffre imaginaire de l'amour purement physique est, si j'ose dire (et je l'ose) un cul de sac! (*Récits*, p. 334).

He is reported as feeling proud (perversely?) of having denied himself, his readers and his young couple the 'partie de jambes en l'air' that so easily and naturally could have happened (IV, 1344). Love, for Giono, is always prehension and comprehension, but the prehension in this novel is reticent, distanced. 'Reserve', however, can mean future provision, as well as decorous retreat. We might perhaps wonder whether Angelo has a low sexual drive, though he later has a child by Pauline. At one point, Pauline taunts him over his lack of surprise at her love-marriage (**446**). Before he meets her, he is indeed troubled, but so might be anyone, by coarse, open sexuality in the inn-mates' 'miaulements de femmes aussi agaçants que ceux des chattes en chasse' (**100**). Men and women there drink copiously, grabbing and rummaging each other: 'Il avait une peur bleue de ces femmes' (**102**). When he returns later, a scene of total carnage greets his gaze. It seems like an authorial chastisement for promiscuity and sexual greed.

With Pauline and Angelo, in the words of *The Song of Solomon*, 'love is as strong as death'. It is certainly as strong a mystery as death. We readers are kept at bay, by a kind of authorial screen, from the unspoken, unconsummated but undeniable love between the two, even though we eye-witness and eavesdrop on their night of love. In a plague-torn world where mistrust seems essential for survival, love is the one untouched, remaining area of total trust, of taking for granted what is granted.

Thinking he has lost her for good, the exhausted Angelo falls asleep on her naked belly. He awakens to hear her calling him 'tu', though he perseveres with 'vous'. Thus she registers their new intimacy. When the crisis is past, they simply, meaningfully, hold hands in mutual gratitude (**495**). When they reach her goal, the haven, she keeps her promise of wearing a long dress during the few days of his stay. He wants both to cover up her recent nakedness and to fix an image of her as entirely, delectably womanly. The husband is still absent. Angelo talks at length to Pauline's mother-in-law of his passion for liberty, which will take him away to Italy. Unlike in the film (to be discussed later), neither he nor Pauline makes any promises, nor does he write to her. Indeed, the novel ends precipitously: Angelo, deliriously happy, returns home. The couple have apparently not consigned themselves to the welcomed, liberating prison-house of love, or, if they have, we have not been informed.

Chapter Two

Politics and beyond

Passionate politics

It is Giuseppe who transmits the letter to Angelo from his mother, in which she flaunts her insolent, passional theory of politics as a thrillingly perilous *divertissement*. Her son inherits much of this attitude, but his foster brother Giuseppe provides a counter-version: political realism.

When Angelo meets him again in the hillside camp near Manosque, Giuseppe strikes him as very different from the man so lovingly remembered and dreamt of during their separation. Giuseppe is by trade a cobbler from Piedmont, like Giono's father. Though he remains attractive to Angelo's eyes, he also seems fishy. All the same, he quite rightly prides himself on being closer to the common man than Angelo, whose batman he had been in the army of the King of Sardinia. The loner Angelo is very disturbed at the iron discipline Giuseppe has set up in the camp, and distinctly unimpressed by his foster brother's new-found fearfulness. With arrogant litotes, Giuseppe declares: 'Je suis un peu dans tout' (**275**). On that hillside he has engineered the re-creation of a little Italy, a Mafia controlling the compliant French bourgeois, who busy themselves arranging urban furniture, knick-knackery, in short, their lives in the open-air of the tented settlement. This is to Angelo's gaze an incongruous spectacle. After the chaos installed by the cholera, Giuseppe, working via delegates and exploiting the catastrophic opportunity, imposes rigid organisation, and appears frankly ready to manipulate others rather than to serve them. *Le Hussard sur le toit* lives off chaos, order, disorders. All Giuseppe's careful programming is disrupted by torrential rain, and new outbreaks of the cholera.

For some years before this novel, Giono had been fascinatedly immersed in the writings of the early Renaissance Florentine political theorist Machiavelli. He once likened criticism of Machiavelli's realism to thieves protesting against street-lighting (IV, 1347-8). For him, Machiavelli forced home unwelcome truths, and lit up obscurantist versions of political reality. If, therefore, Giuseppe follows the ideas of his illustrious compatriot, Giono is not automatically condemning him in comparison with the obviously much more idealistic Angelo. For Giuseppe, expediency is all: 'Notre devoir étant de gagner, il faut garder toutes les chances; et même les fausses cartes' (**263**). He is prepared for dirty tricks and dirty hands. Unwittingly, he all but got his beloved Angelo killed, for he had spread anti-government rumours around Manosque, which resulted in the hanging of several citizens, and created the climate of paranoia which nearly led to Angelo being lynched. Refreshing his face at the public fountain in Manosque, Angelo had suddenly been grabbed by a mob and denounced as a government agent sent to poison water supplies. In other words, an *agent provocateur* seeking to incriminate the government for sabotage. Giono was inventing nothing here, for once: such rumours did circulate during the epidemic, including one claiming that the cholera itself was a government plot to reduce the size of the population. Angelo's captors are workers. One, described in a male stereotype as hysterical like a woman, is Michu, Giuseppe's man in Manosque. It is a gendarme who rescues Angelo from lynching. Angelo thinks the false anti-authority rumours 'une lâcheté' (**125**), though he has no love for constituted governments. Giono in all this exhibits no knee-jerk fondness for the working-class, no hatred of the forces of law and order. What interests him is the phenomenon of xenophobia, and the consequent victimisation of scapegoats.

Angelo prefers duels to political assassinations; in this he is instinctively anti-Machiavellian. His aristocratic anarchism, his cult of self-reliance, are summed up when he tells Pauline: 'On ne se fait pas l'âme par personnes interposées' (**446**). But how can you have politics without proxies? Though he himself will be utilised by politicians as a straw man in *Le Bonheur fou*, he loathes, unlike the delegating Giuseppe, the very concept of middlemen. He is largely a soloist, *un franc-tireur*. Though politically naive, he knows revolutions can go bad, can simply reinstall a different form of tyranny (**138**). He puts his finger on the paradox at the heart of all would-be emancipation movement: 'Devenir leur maître pour leur donner la liberté?' (**141**). He feels that he could in fact replace the word 'freedom' with another, so long as it was *'aussi vague'* (**206**; Giono's emphasis). He can see an analogy between revolution and the epidemic. Both turn society upside down; both can bring out the worst and the best in individuals. The huge difference, of course, is that revolution at least promises to give a chance to life.

On the hillside, witnessing a religious gathering 'en train de demander simplement à tous les saints de prier pour eux', Angelo makes a wry but pointed joke: 'Cela doit faire forcément recette. Il faudrait trouver en politique un truc semblable. S'il n'existe pas déjà, il faut l'inventer': prayers in lieu of voting (**239**). Incidentally, the music in this rite lifts him out of his current concerns: 'La musique créait un monde sans politique où le choléra n'était plus qu'un exercice de style' (**240**). In this respect, as no doubt in others, music and love are interchangeable: both escape from, and contradict, the horrors of this world. Angelo, besides, has many moments of doubt about a political vocation:

> «Peuple, je t'aime!» dit Angelo à haute voix. Mais tout de suite il eut scrupule et il se demanda si en réalité il n'aimait pas le peuple comme on aime le poulet. (**295**)

He loathes the idea of revolution becoming institutionalised, bureaucratised, confiscated from those it is supposed to serve.

He does not evolve in linear fashion from political naivety to realism, from Ariosto to Machiavelli. The two tendencies coexist and alternate, depending on the individual qualities of those he encounters, and his own morale and moods. This variability offsets the woolly nature of his ideology. Giuseppe, anyway, is also vague, mysterious: 'Il va falloir que tu ailles où il faut faire ce que tu sais' (**268**). In the old days, they engaged in frequent near-lethal duels, followed by instant reconciliations, in which they fell into each other's arms. In the hillside camp, after much disagreement over political pragmatism and Angelo's deep disappointment over the changes come about in Giuseppe, they fight again, bloodily, with bare knuckles, and Angelo is the victor. Though he will never stop loving him, the later killing of his brother (in *Le Bonheur fou*) is foreshadowed here.

There are potential parallels in *Le Hussard sur le toit* with the postwar period of French history: the murderous political correctness of 1944-1945, the purges of the Liberation, the settling of old scores, and the crimes committed by opportunists of every or no political hue. As the gendarme says: 'si vous avez besoin d'assassins prenez toujours des froussards' (**124**). On a more personal level, Giono firmly believed that the French Communist Party was behind his arrest in late 1944. Always hostile to party-mindedness, he called them 'les *Karl Marx brothers*' (IV, 1348). In the novel, Giuseppe's band stands roughly for the Communists.

As it feeds on the struggle against oppression (the cholera is 'natural', but exacerbated and cashed in on by human intervention), *Le Hussard sur le toit* is inherently political. Choices of side have to be made, or abstention followed through. Responsibility—individual, civic, official—lies at the heart of the drama. In *Le Bonheur fou,* the epidemic will mutate into murderous chicanery. Giono's instinctive reaction is to exclaim: a plague on *all* your houses. Yet the fascination with the whole repellent phenomenon of politics was always there. In *Naissance de l'Odyssée,* Ulysses learns the profitability of self-projection, image-making. Machiavelli punctures illusions. Both Ulysses and Machiavelli, in their divergent ways, pursue impregnability, which is also the dream of the temperamental anarchist. The tone of Giono's latter-day discourse, apparently cynical, is just a different kind of eyewash, like many literary or indeed everyday disclaimers. At least eyewash is better than brainwashing.

Nature

It is tempting to polarise, and to say that the previous Arcadia of Giono's fictional country becomes, in *Le Hussard sur le toit,* a hell on earth; but it was never, except at rare high points, Arcadia. A long section of *Que ma joie demeure* achieves Dionysiac bliss, a desiring harmony among human beings, nature and the beasts of the field. Just as often, however, Giono recognises the insuperable otherness of the physical world, as in the text 'La Grande Barrière', even though elsewhere he makes numerous attempts to abolish barriers, to humanise nature, just as he always strove to renaturalise human society. In his work, comparisons of people to animals are almost always non-pejorative, even meliorative. In *Le Hussard sur le toit,* the opposite of the free manoeuvres craved by Angelo and Pauline are barricades, *cordons sanitaires,* locked doors. These are also, of course, normal human attempts to counter the plague, but Giono sees fit to disparage them as futile and even counter-productive. There was always a recurrent apocalyptic vision in Giono's work: not so much a nuclear winter as a modern world suddenly shunted back to its early days; wild boars emerge, blinking, from the Métro which has reverted to being a lair. The question is: how would human beings cope with the challenge of a revirginised world? Sartre's *La Nausée* picks up on this vision of nature overturning and overgrowing man-made structures.

In this novel, the sun, normally the source of all life, seems to be siding with death: asphyxiating humans, animals and plants with paranormal heat, and accelerating decay and further infection. The transmogrified countryside forewarns Angelo of the advent of cholera. Everything is out of joint. Things are melting, coming apart at the seams, drying up, losing their usual contours and hence their definition and character. Nature is alien, no longer at man's disposal. It is intensely dead, and so, curiously, alive. If a sensible person is never blindly confident face to face with natural forces, here she or he has every reason to feel completely unsure and everywhere threatened. Nature is now a monster, unnatural. Criss-crosses operate: as the epidemic evolves and spreads, people become, in their desperation, more animal-like, and animals more people-like, if not human.

Le Poids du ciel had earlier, both in its title and obsessively in its text, propounded an overarching image of a weighty heavens to which human beings were urged to open themselves physically and imaginatively. It is not there the Baudelairean image of a ponderous sky pressing down on humanity, like a casserole lid forcing the denizens of this earth to stew in their own postlapsarian juice.[5] In *Le Hussard sur le*

[5] 'Spleen' ('Quand le ciel bas et lourd...'), in *Les Fleurs du mal,* ed. G. Chesters (Bristol Classical Press, 1995), pp. 73-4.

toit, though without the theological input, heat and light, likewise, exert intolerable pressure downwards. More particularly, enormous clouds of butterflies pressurise everything on which they settle (**366**). Here as elsewhere, Giono revels in correcting or upturning cosy received ideas. He stresses the salaciousness of doves, or the sadism of nightingales—not that any orthodox morality governs such terms in his usage. Always fascinated by bestiaries—fantastic as well as zoological—Giono, like Hitchcock in *The Birds*, orchestrates a massive takeover by our feathered friends. Like dogs or pigs, birds loot, capitalising on the rich pickings of human carrion.

Especially crows, or ravens (which share the same name in French and which do in fact belong to the same genus). In mythologies and religions the world over and from time immemorial, crows have embodied ill-omen, intelligence, and death. In idiomatic French, *corbeau* connotes: (1) priests (the black garb); (2) those who cart off corpses in epidemics, or body-snatchers; (3) anybody of ill omen; (4) a rapacious person; and (5) a writer of poison-pen letters. We have already seen Giuseppe's covert and underhand use of political denunciation at work. Giono sets a crow feasting on the cornea of a dead woman (**49**). An inquisition of crows eyeball Angelo on the roof: 'de petits yeux d'or, sinon méchants, en tout cas extraordinairement froids' (**147**). Angelo himself is called 'un corbeau' when he helps to collect cadavers in Giuseppe's camp (**282**). If he had a dark side, it might emerge in the guise of the crow that tries to 'rape' Pauline.

Not all God's creatures are dangerous enemies. On the roofs, Angelo enjoys the loyal company of a cat, though naturally he wonders what it has been feeding on, and whether it carries the cholera in its strokable fur. The cat dogs him, and is a rare reassurance of normality amid all the abnormality of the epidemic. Despite his keen sensitivity to natural sights, smells, sounds, which he reads for pure pleasure as well as for traveller's information, Angelo confesses to Pauline:

> ... que puis-je faire avec un hêtre au bout de cinq minutes de compagnie avec lui? Je me dis qu'il est beau, je me le répète deux ou trois fois, je prends plaisir à sa beauté puis il faut que je passe à autre chose, dans quoi il y a l'homme. (**351**)

Much more distanced is the opinion of an elderly gent in a quarantine:

> *Si Pâris avait vu la peau d'Hélène telle qu'elle était,* dit le vieux monsieur, *il aurait aperçu un réseau gris-jaune, inégal, rude* [...]; *jamais il n'aurait été amoureux d'Hélène. La nature est un grand opéra dont les décorations font un effet d'optique.* (96)

According to Giono, this last phrase was perhaps from Pierre Bayle, but Giono was extremely fond of inventing quotations, in a kind of reverse plagiarism which foists instead of stealing. These two citations would seem to indicate a change of heart on Giono's part, were it not for the great wealth of nature descriptions which people his work, including *Le Hussard sur le toit*, right up to the end. The second quotation does point the way to the gripping encounter with the hermit-doctor, whose extravagant, poetical philosophising is the true climax of the novel. The doctor's discourse will gloss the plague in all its verbal glory, just before Angelo saves Pauline from the cholera, the one instance of such rescue in the whole novel.

Chapter Three

Pandemic meanings

Reading symbols can be either reductive, or like standing perilously on shifting sands. Reductively, we could read *Le Hussard sur le toit* as an allegory of the Second World War (*La Peste* has been similarly headshrunk). A country lies helplessly under siege by an alien power. In one sector, the infected ones are compelled to wear a stigmatic cross, as Jews were branded with the Star of David in Occupied France. Some collaborate with the disease (and the German storm troopers were called 'la peste brune'); some resist; and many of both persuasions lose their lives. Food shortages, black markets, internment camps, scapegoating, all these factors link Giono's novel with the historical reality of the 1939-1945 War.

Before the war and before Camus's plague novel, Antonin Artaud had published his provocative, influential essay, 'Le Théâtre et la Peste' (in *Le Théâtre et son double,* 1935), in which he metaphorises plague:

> Le théâtre, comme la peste, est une crise qui se dénoue par la mort ou par la guérison [...], poussant les hommes à se voir tels qu'ils sont, elle fait tomber le masque, elle découvre le mensonge, la veulerie, la bassesse, la tartuferie.

In this perspective, the plague acts as a catalyst or demiurge:

> La peste prend des images qui dorment, un désordre latent et les pousse tout à coup jusqu'aux gestes les plus extrêmes; et le théâtre aussi prend les gestes et les pousse à bout.[6]

In Giono's text, in the doctor's version of events, human beings themselves are, like Artaud's plague / theatre, bitter-enders, possessed by a (demonic?) logic. As nature ceaselessly plays and experiments with itself, so people exploit their own

---

[6] A. Artaud, 'Le Théâtre et la Peste'. *Œuvres complètes* (Gallimard, 1964), IV, 39; 34.

potentialities, beyond conventional good and evil, come hell or high water. The human body in the grip of cholera is held to be taking over from reason, and beginning to reason in its own methodically mad way. As with Artaud's vision, nothing in Giono's is skeletal, desiccated allegory, nor is the plague symbol annexable to a Christian perspective. The body is a densely rich enough mystery; why speak of the soul?

Many European languages foster the phonetic collision or overlap of 'cosmic' and 'comic'. Giono and Artaud stand some distance from the Camus of *La Peste*. It is true that Angelo at one point 'se demanda tout à coup s'il n'y avait, quelque part, mêlée à l'univers, une énorme plaisanterie' (**82**). At this moment, the generally unlugubrious Angelo is thinking in terms of a supremely bad joke played by a puppeteer God or Trickster, amusing Himself in the unutterable boredom of His infinity with a grotesque and homicidal pantomime. (A similar view plays a more central part in Giono's *Le Moulin de Pologne*, in which an ill-starred family undergoes a whole epidemic of arbitrary deaths.) All of this is far less solemn than *La Peste*, and absurdity hovers instead of Absurdity. Like a good pagan, Giono can afford to be relaxed about God in a way Camus never was.

It is fairly easy to nitpick Camus's symbolism. The bubonic plague is not, like war, man-made. The medical squads cannot stand for the Maquis, as they try to save life whereas the latter had often to take it. Neither is the plague an adequate allegorical carrier of evil, as *La Peste* puts on show an unnamed, external force punishing a largely blameless population. The feel-good ending (Dr Rieux concluding that there is more to admire than to condemn in his fellow-citizens) is not truly supported by the preceding evidence of the text, where only a select few behave admirably. Camus's plague-symbol is both too much and not enough, too all-embracing, and yet insufficiently substantiated. In contrast, Giono denies himself the opportunity for sentimentalism offered by the death of children. His juvenile corpses are, as they should be, on the same level as adult ones:

> Les petits cadavres étaient semblables aux cadavres des grandes personnes, c'est-à-dire d'une indécence ridicule, *criants de vérité...* (**192**; Giono's emphasis)

The two novels do draw closer together in the stoical idea of perfectly useless activity, Sisyphean obduracy. In Camus's work, Meursault in atomised fashion, and Dr Rieux in focussed mode, answer an absurd fate with gratuitous behaviour, as Angelo does in company with the nun and the young doctor. Both Giono's and Camus's novels seek to administer, in their different ways, a profound jolt to that 'stupide confiance humaine' that *La Peste* evokes. Yet overall, the repressed rhetoric and the half-smothered lyricism of Camus are not Giono's way: he fires both barrels.

The hermit-doctor's version

The major shot at a rounded reading of the epidemic is let off in the long confrontation between the two young refugees and an aging hermit-doctor-scholar. Even he, however, does not so much explicate as complicate the total phenomenon. Despite his hectoring rhetoric, does he truly want to proselytise, to convert the green hopefuls? 'Je suis bien loin de vouloir vous faire un laïus' (**469**). Retired from medical practice, he has had acres of time in which to muse and embroider: he is out of the action from which the couple have escaped only temporarily.

Angelo and Pauline arrive at this refuge in a downpour. It is a kind of Noah's Ark, with a flood all around and three survivors on board (the beasts of the field are taking care of themselves very nicely). This image prepares for the theme of voyages later in the scene. The travelling pair enter a room littered with books and pell-mell furniture: a maze with an enigmatic, fabulating, if very open, creature at the heart of it. Angelo feels deep embarrassment over his nudity in front of Pauline as he dries himself. The doctor, who has seen it all, mocks Angelo's blushes by a reference to the episode in Rousseau's *Confessions* where a Venetian courtesan wittily suggests to a Jean-Jacques put off his stroke by the sight of her asymmetric breasts that, if he can't cope with imperfect women, he should take up trigonometry (**465**). Angelo will often feel in the ensuing scene that he is being re-stripped bare by the bluff, scouring words of his host. Reassuringly, the powerfully seductive smell of a *daube* cooking reminds Angelo that, *pace* Ariosto and other verbal magicians, 'c'est dans la réalité qu'on est la plupart du temps' (**461**). Fully dressed again, he boosts his morale by reflecting that «Être dans ses bottes [...] est peut-être le fin mot de la puissance» (**466**): living, and dying if need be, with his boots on, ready for anything. He puffs one of his cherished cheroots: 'Il n'y a pas de petit plaisir' (**467**), Giono's lifelong lesson that we all knew already off by heart. Angelo watches his lady companion, in many ways a more physical creature than he, wolfing the solid food neither has had for days:

> ... la jeune femme dévorait de façon brutale et même [...] elle ne pouvait s'empêcher de pousser quelques petits gémissements. D'ailleurs, elle fermait les yeux. (**467**)

The doctor begins his discourse with seeming modesty:

> Discernement parfait, tranché, élémentaire et jamais en défaut dès qu'il s'agit des sens. Or, les sens s'exercent dans l'immédiat. De là, mon humilité. (**468**)

The first of these sentences is already an arrogant claim. He can only be a stand-in for Giono when he proposes: 'Si je prends la peine de vous parler du choléra vous serez étonné' (**469**), for Giono devoted his life to gobsmacking readers. Also Gionesque is his cavalier way with the word 'liar': 'Était-il besoin de dire qu'il n'attachait pas au mot menteur un sens péjoratif, loin de là?' (**471**). This ploy is meant to soften up his listeners and Giono's readers for an acceptance of *invention* (which usefully means both discovery and fabrication). Nothing he will say can be proved, or indeed disproved. No anatomical dissection would reveal what 'really' happens in the poetic innards of human beings, in the doctor's version 'la foudre bleuâtre plein de paons sauvages de la jouissance' (**472**). His diagnosis will be substantially erotic. Though he makes an anachronistic allusion to Claude Bernard's researches on the liver, made public only in 1853, his whole attitude to science is one of leaving fact for dead. Reality is a pre-text and a pretext: starting-blocks to take off from.

The doctor's amplification moves through varying criteria and categories. One is ethical, though as always with Giono, unorthodoxly so. In this perspective, the discourse is less fanciful, sticks closer to feasible facts. Thus:

> C'est comique [...]. Nous avons une épidémie de peur. Actuellement, si j'appelle choléra un brassard jaune et si je le fais porter à mille personnes, les mille crèvent en quinze jours. (**462**)

This is autosuggestion on a grand scale, which will be his major theme, but, at this stage, it is of a non-proactive nature. (It is also, of course, a callously sardonic reference to the marking of Jews in Occupied France). Linked with funk is egocentricity. While, maybe grudgingly, acknowledging the factual cholera ('Je sais fort bien que le choléra n'est pas tout à fait le produit de l'imagination pure' [*ibid.*]), the doctor is most excited by the exasperation of this scientific fact by 'le fameux égoïsme congénital. On meurt littéralement d'égoïsme' (*ibid.*). When Angelo tries to counter with the example of the young French doctor, the hermit blocks by claiming that this unusual individual was perhaps *too* good (to be true?): 'Il faut une mesure en tout. Mais donnez-moi simplement quelqu'un qui *s'oublie*' (**463**; Giono's emphasis). ('S'oublier' is also a euphemism for involuntary excretion, 'to have an accident', which all cholera victims are constrained to have).

What about a variant form of self-centredness: melancholy, *ennui*? ('*Chol*era' and 'melan*chol*ia' have a common root: bile). For his own part, the doctor lays claim to 'mélancolie, mais pas misanthropie' (**464**). He speaks knowledgeably of 'le délire de l'inutilité', and of 'les démesures de néant' (*ibid.*), but maintains he has escaped such ravages with the help of Victor Hugo (**465**). Some corpses seen by Angelo have indeed seemed sunk in topical spleen:

> [Ils] avaient surtout le mal du siècle: une certaine nonchalance d'allure et mélancolie d'attitude, l'air d'en avoir assez, une sorte de mépris de bonne compagnie. (**421**)

Even here, Giono cannot resist enlivening the sorrowful state. In many other of his fictions, the frequent suicides or murders seem similarly to have more to do with a strange, terminal, active lust for 'divertissement' than with static depression. Giono can, it is true, at times invoke a more passive temptation to accept the invitation offered by death, as in the phenomenon of vertigo, suffered briefly by Angelo himself on the roofs of Manosque, when he feels sucked towards the abyss. Giono was probably the least likely person to carry out suicide, but he was in the vanguard of those who contemplate, nay *entertain,* the idea of suicide, and see its attractions. Increasingly favouring, as he aged, 'divertissement' of any and every variety, Giono was anti-Pascalian. For Pascal, a life of *divertissement* is a sinful distraction from the duty of thinking of death. For Giono, life—not to be confined under the labels of 'sinful' or 'virtuous'—can find distraction *in* death, the last great spectacle before the curtain comes down for good.

Giono bestows on the doctor his own (and Angelo's, described several times as 'fasciné') curiosity about the epidemic, which is what of course made him originally dive into all that documentation on it. Whereas most of us are afraid of or incurious about extinction and, as Pascal complained, avert our gazes, Giono's *ennui* is never incurious. Suicide means choosing your own moment of death: it is an act of will. We should note the contrast in this sentence between passive and proactive nouns: ' Il [le choléra] ne se transmet pas par contagion mais *par prosélytisme'* (**471-2**; Giono's emphasis). Outside this novel, Giono's people, not just the select few but also the common run, are so wilful that they want to will even their own death.[7] In suicide, self-destruction is the obverse face of self-affirmation or self-preservation. It is a resolutely Godless theology.

'Le cholérique n'est pas un patient, *c'est un impatient'* (**478**; Giono's emphasis). This pointed pun opens up the question to embrace the rush towards death. In Baudelaire's 'Le Voyage', the poet claims that the lust for new experience is worth any price, any sacrifice, any plunge into horror. The doctor's version is to see the human body itself as such an expanse of amazing novelty: 'Le foie est semblable à un extraordinaire océan, où la sonde ne touche jamais le fond' (**470**). *Sonde* is both a nautical lead-line and a medical probe. In *Fragments d'un paradis* (1948), the crew of the ship *L'Indien* sail off to

---

[7] Or that of others, as in murder. Langlois, in *Un roi sans divertissement* (1947), which adapts Pascal's famous phrase for its own purposes, or the narrator of *Les Grands Chemins* (1951), both practise loving, violent euthanasia to put murderous others out of their misery.

explore whether 'la réalité est plus fantastique que l'imagination' (III, 967). In Giono, this binary pair are never polar opposites but, rather, interactive. As in ancient divination, the doctor reads the entrails. At the start of *Le Hussard sur le toit*, a naval physician performs an autopsy on an infected ship's topman. He lays bare an anatomical universe, 'bourré comme un pot à feu' (**41**). Although his report lacks the astounding 'metaphysical', moral and poetic extensions or escalations of the hermit's version, it still betrays an awareness of the huge-in-the-small: 'il y a ici une bombe capable de faire en cinq sec éclater le royaume comme une grenade sanguinolente' (*ibid.*). This is a premonition of the cataclysmic impact of the coming epidemic, whereas for the hermit the body is a New World, across and through which the imagination can make fabulous voyages. Drug addicts, mystics, but also persons in the street if they have vicarious curiosity, would instinctively understand this variant kind of out-of-body experience, centred though it is in the body.

But of course curiosity killed the cat. It may be open-ended, but it must have an end. Curiosity has no core, no preconceptions; it takes us where it wills. One of Giono's favourite refrains is: 'On se perd en conjectures', though such losing is more akin to self-discovery, or at least self-invention. The doctor's theory is largely psychosomatic. People will cholera on themselves. Although this sounds far-fetched to commonsense, we might think of those groups who commit mass harakiri. What were they dying towards? Within the novel, the rough-tongued nun, in much shorter space, counters in advance the bluff doctor. In both cases, Angelo climbs down from his high horse. The nun fights the rush to die. She lives by the existential pun: 'J'approprie' (I make them fit [to meet their maker], I clean them up). She is dynamic, the doctor imaginatively stationary, 'un voyageur immobile', as Giono was lifelong. It is a luxury position.

The doctor, however, oscillates. At different moments, he exalts or belittles the body or human sentiments. The whole speech is expansive, not reductive. He is not arguing, like many nineteenth-century scientists, that all we are is a series of substances and chemical reactions (our contemporary version: we are, temporarily, only superior computers). He marvels at, worships, that which he summons up from the depths. It is not the anatomy of melancholy but of wonderment. He is in addition totally unconcerned about what other medicos would say of him: 'Il s'était naturellement fait traiter d'esprit non scientifique et même d'âne bâté' (**470**).

In order to underline his own confidence in his vision, he can afford to allow for last-minute swerves into prosaic doubt on the part of the hungerers after the sublime that he has been evoking. The *cholérique* might pull up *in extremis*, feeling he is going too far, and wondering 's'il ne valait pas mieux manger son pot-au-feu [as the three of them have just done] sans penser à Charlemagne' (**483**). The doctor also thinks against himself on the subject of love. Despite having said earlier that cholera is not an illness, *'c'est un sursaut d'orgueil'* (**473**; Giono's emphasis), which would conclusively rule out any part for love in the whole affair, for 'le cholérique *suit son idée*' (**476**; Giono's emphasis), a monomaniac activity, he later admits that the only remedy against the killer 'serait d'être préféré' (**479**). He goes on:

> ... il faudrait se faire préférer, offrir plus que ne donne ce sursaut d'orgueil: en un mot *être plus fort, ou plus beau, ou plus séduisant que la mort.* (**480**; Giono's emphasis)

Though it is unwarranted to speak of cause and effect in this instance, this intervention is exactly what Angelo will achieve in the following chapter, when his love, devotion and self-abnegation (*s'oublier*) yank Pauline back from the persuasive call of death, as he had earlier comforted her after the simulated rape by the amorous crow that battened on her. If we can will death, we can also nill it. Love above all proves, even more than the powers of imagination eulogised by the doctor throughout his speech, that 'nous sommes en réalité beaucoup plus que nous ne croyons' (**483**). Generous love, that two-seat Utopia, can replace the solitary ecstasy, the self-defeating triumph, which the doctor maintains can be achieved by *cholériques*. If Angelo's saving of Pauline is orgasmic, then lovers oppose such 'little death' (as the Elizabethans termed sexual climax) to the great big one awaiting us all.

André Breton had laid down the (Surrealist) law in 1928: 'La beauté sera CONVULSIVE ou ne sera pas'.[8] The key terms in

---

[8] A. Breton: *Nadja* (Le Livre de poche, 1964 [1928]), p. 187.

the doctor's discourse are: explosion, fireworks, sun ('Quel beau feu d'artifice!' [473]), peacocks, flight, voyages, ocean. His style is pyrotechnic. His words seek to match the firework display of death in all its inhuman glory: words against the apocalypse. Fireworks, of course, light up the heavens only briefly, and then darkness redescends. And such verbal exuberance is only, perhaps, sublimely decorative: 'Une hypertrophie de la fioriture' (*ibid.*), baroque into rococo. Yet the young pair (and the reader, putatively) are entranced, as can happen when a writer indulges himself with total lack of abashedness. This is the Giono of *Noé* admitting proudly: 'Je prends en ce moment un grand plaisir à l'aventure de la phrase' (III, 684). The free association propelling the doctor's words is the polar opposite of that political discipline with which Angelo would like to be, if only that were possible, freely associated.

The older man's fable seeks to rewrite, or add previously hidden depths to, the younger man's hands-on experience of cholera. The cholera: a very large part of Giono's total wordage in *Le Hussard dans le toit*—a novel on, and in, the plague. The cholera: the doctor's verbal epidemic, the imaginary, enormous microcosm within the macrocosm of the whole novel. The doctor's version of the plague brings back human self-affirmation, passion and wonderment into an equation in which their opposites had seemed to rule the roost. Is this new and late-in-the-day effort futile, self-deluding, but heartening? We should never discount the humour in this speech. Does the doctor mean all he says? Humour, too, invites us to rethink, to view from another angle, to refuse the obvious. The doctor's amused philosophy, sometimes self-contradictory pot-pourri though it be, interiorises the physical world. In his gaze, human beings are microcosms and macrocosms. He opens up the body and, like an explorer, the world.

On a more geopolitical level, the lure of death is a constant theme in Giono's aversion to much in modern civilisation: the mass suicide represented by war; the rape and murder of the environment; the loss of self-belief and self-reliance that leads to readiness to abdicate personal responsibility, and to acquiesce in or even worship totalitarian systems. Even so, and even when enraged or amused by human folly, the writer in

Giono (and was there much else?) can only welcome a release of energy, however crazy in effect. The plague *is* beneficial, as Artaud proposed. If the cholera is pure hyperbole, then some, like the hermit, react hyperbolically. Talk about the cholera proliferates like the cholera itself. Colic, cholera: spasmic rhythms, disordered flow, letting go, running wild (Angelo is a fairly constipated, stiff-necked young man).

Finally, for Jacques Chabot in his incisive essay on *Le Hussard sur le toit*, the cholera, which magnetises so much talk, cannot or does not need to be explicated definitively. It is tautegorical, self-explanatory: 'Il se parle lui-même'.[9] It is true that no critic has, as yet, come up with a totally satisfying analysis and evaluation of the hermit-doctor section, very probably because it would be impossible to do so, undecidable in ways Derrida hardly dreamt of. Hard though it be to admit defeat, I have to say that this rhapsodic discourse dazzles, troubles, opens up far-flung possibilities, but any critical closure is out of the question. We can parse but not totalise this section. Such an extremist monologue (the young pair remain mesmerised) no doubt breeds in different readers extremes of response, from finding it frenzied gibberish at one end, to unblinking plunge into the heart of the matter at the other.

In *Le Foulard de Smyrne*, a pedlar, always invisible under an outsize blue umbrella, spreads the cholera via his wares. In the novel, the doctor, first encountered under a similar blue umbrella, proceeds to spread the cholera. That is: to extend its meaning, to infiltrate it into the core of imaginative and passional life. Perhaps no human agency can tame the epidemic, reduce it to verbal schemes, but it is well worth a go at stylishly matching it, imitating it, and in the process humanising it.

For Pierre Citron, Giono's biographer and the cornucopious provider of ideas and notes in the Pléiade edition of the novel, this section is Giono let loose, veering between rational argument and surrealism. He lists the alternations, the conflicts, the coexistences in the doctor's monologue:

> ... son bon sens de bourgeois rationaliste et matérialiste, sa brutalité, sa vulgarité d'expression. Sa finesse d'analyse et de perception, ses paradoxes, son délire de sorcier goguenard qui

---

[9] J. Chabot, *L'Humeur belle* (Publications de l'Université de Provence, 1992), p. 150.

> semble faire surgir l'irréel de l'excès même du réel, ses conventions de langage et la hardiesse de ses images poétiques, l'imbrication linguistiquement étonnante du discours direct et du discours indirect libre dans ses propos non seulement d'une phrase à l'autre mais jusqu'à l'intérieur d'une même phrase. (IV, 1364-5)

In setting up this confrontation of a retired oldster and an active young man, Giono is, for Chabot, not only having his cake and eating it, but mocking what he still hugs to his heart: 'L'homme d'expérience s'amuse à taquiner en lui-même une juvénile naïveté dont il n'a pas encore fini de se départir.' The hermit might be past it, but his imagination can still run riot. Giono projected a text called *Fêtes de la mort*, a title which could usefully fit the doctor's contribution.

Chapter Four

Style: home industry and foreign aid

Style is of crucial importance to Angelo. Dress, habits, modes of address, attitudes to situations: all must have a certain pronounced style. Beyond Angelo, death by cholera needs to be confronted by a range of styles, for style is a uniquely human phenomenon. By it we answer back, affirm ourselves against all that is not ourselves. Angelo opposes his enlarging gaze to the hyperbole of the epidemic: 'tu démesures. [...] Tu es inguérissable: l'œil collé à la loupe, la bouche au porte-voix' (**236-7**). Giono himself of course constantly exaggerates, or indeed rewrites reality: 'Le soleil était si violent qu'il leur [aux corbeaux] blanchissait les plumes' (**215**). While any writer, or human in general, houses and evicts words, Giono spends his verbal money like a drunken sailor. He animates, dynamises, all he touches. He makes the ethereal fat: 'La lumière était très blanche et tellement écrasée qu'elle semblait beurrer la terre avec un air épais' (**13**). Later, the air is so compacted that it is necessary to bend down to see under it (**272**). He reinvents dendrology: 'Les forêts fondaient comme des blocs de lard' (**32**). Giono rarely records; he adds, piles it on thick: 'Les formes se déformaient dans un air visqueux comme du sirop' (**27**). It is essentially a torrential style, accumulative, and clobbering the reader with multiple sense impressions. As he wrote in his pacifist pamphlet *Refus d'obéissance*:

> J'ai voulu saouler tout le monde de vie. J'aurais voulu pouvoir faire bouillonner la vie comme un torrent, [...] assommer [les hommes] de fraîcheur [...] et les emporter dans le torrent. (*Récits*, p. 264).

Just as Giono is untroubled by mixed metaphor as he marches confidently from one comparison to another, so his sense of the grotesque *mixes it*. Hybrids, monsters, always appealed to him. An anti-classic, a Romantic, he breaks down barriers, genres, registers. From his very first writings, his escalating imagery (Panturle's misshapen lip in *Regain* likened to a whole red pepper) teetered on the verge of the caricatural. At times in *Le Hussard sur le toit*, with its dying people reduced to disarticulated, robotic dummies, Giono appears to second Bergson's over-famous mechanics of humour: 'Du mécanique plaqué sur du vivant'.[10] His comic range, however, is wider. He concocts humorous situations, so that, as in Ariosto or Cervantes, the mock-heroic and parody cohabit with chivalric exaltation. A sentinel helps Angelo to escape, in a parody of adventure novels, from the quarantine over which he is supposed to be standing guard; and he gives Angelo so much gen that the latter is totally confused (**99**). Giono is ready to skit his hero. When, on the basis of natural noises, Angelo imagines a whole world, his author chastises him for his over-fanciful detective work: 'Le pays n'avait aucun rapport avec celui qu'Angelo avait imaginé' (**315**). This might also be Giono's wry joke at his own expense, for what has he ever done except invent whole countries?

In this novel, this Dance of Death, Giono is as funny about death as about life, though the two apparent opposites curiously feed each other. At the heart of the epidemic spectacle, are the impatient patients doubled up with frenzied laughter or excruciating colic? A corpse can display a grin, the rictus; is it in death-throes or the throes of laughter? Giono wanted his novel to be 'cocasse': a scream (IV, 1140, n. 2). Despite the physical horrors Angelo plunges into and the melancholy fits he at times succumbs to, *brio giocoso* is the dominant mode and tempo. People's words and facial expressions are ironic, sarcastic, sardonic, as they die in double-quick time.

Giono animates, and reanimates. He twists and recycles clichés, proverbs, idioms. Angelo explains his seeming immunity: 'La contagion me craint comme la peste' (**334**). This wry joke is a kind of double-take which turns a set expression, and Angelo's adversary, back on itself. If you revivify what is dead in language by an act of linguistic voodoo, you are

---

[10] *Le Rire* (Presses Universitaires de France, 1975 [1900]), p. 29.

making a gesture against death, a possibly impotent but heartening V-sign. When he utters rough trooper's oaths, Angelo 'peste'. Conversely, death strips the figurative back to the literal, the pompous to the denuded: victims do shit themselves with fear. Reconverting the ready-made counters *le prêt-à-penser*, colloquial vim can scrub encrusted language. Giono spoke of his fondness for 'le contraste, à mon sens très savoureux, de l'emploi alterné de l'argot et de l'envol'.[11]

Puns play their dramatic part. There is a pointed pun on *colère/choléra* (and the two have etymological kinship): something churning up inside that cries to be spewed forth. Angelo recalling his duel with Baron Swartz lists the components: 'raison, logique et tout le tremblement et sang-froid' (**158**). A knees-knocking iciness; three apparently precise nouns and a blurring one: the whole caboodle. Irony acts as a prophylactic, a verbal sanitary cordon. Irony can, however, cut both ways. Giono fortunately takes his cue from Stendhal on occasion in making his hero on occasion frankly ridiculous. This distancing is obviously intended to short-circuit sentimentality. So Angelo joshes himself and Giono mocks Angelo: a double distancing. In the relationship between Angelo and Pauline, style, rhetoric, emotion are interchangeable: unconsummated desire, the distance between intimates.

What of the faults, excesses, misjudgments of Giono's style? Some of the dialogue is clever-clever, *marivaudage*, for instance the over-allusive exchange between the gendarmes (**123**). Often in this novel, speech conceals as often as it reveals; it is less communication than verbal duelling. Various critics have spoken of Giono's gnomic prolixity, that paradox of so many words used to hide or confuse rather than to clarify. Much play has been made of the opposite stylistic poles: the *enflure* of *le style vicomte* (that lush orotundity associated with Chateaubriand) and *le vernis* (the non-obscuring, glossy plainness) of *le style lieutenant* (Stendhal). In fact, Giono oscillates, overlaps, backslides. All in all, however, he proves in *Le Hussard sur le toit* that an old dog can teach himself new tricks. The fact remains that there is much excess windbaggage, diarrhetoric. The born fabulator is addicted to the *galéjade* (blarney), the angler's tall tales (*histoires*

---

[11] Giono's preface to a free adaptation of Joost van den Vondel's play, *Joseph à Dothan* (Gallimard, 1959), p. 143.

marseillaises), both credited to Meridional writers. *Le Hussard sur le toit*, in addition to informing and enlarging us, seeks to have us on. One such (suggestive) yarn concerns the genesis of this novel. It was born, said Giono, of trains galloping past in the night; their clicking wheels begat clashing sabres (*IV*, 1115). This might even be, approximately, true. Anything can engender anything.

Klaxons can modulate into hunting horns, into French horns. Giono often spoke of his envy of music, its ability to pull together, to counterpoint, whereas words string things out. Giono shared Stendhal's passion for Mozart; the clarinettist encountered by the voyaging couple plays his German dances (**433**). In *Le Hussard sur le toit*, Giono wanted to 'faire du Mozart' (IV, 1137; 1334). Musically literate critics have argued that this novel has the classical structure of a Mozartian concerto; an opening allegro, a middle adagio, and a final presto. In his descriptions of the convulsions of the dying, or fortissimo storms, Giono wanted to score the '"coups de gong" de la nature' (IV, 1334).

Be that as it may, *movement* is obviously inherent in an action-novel. Flight and pursuit: death hounds people, who flee even with their last gasp—running on the spot. The phrase 'à tombeau ouvert' is a grave expression for breakneck speed. The movement, naturally, takes place inevitably within limits: barriers, quarantines, suspended life on roofs. Angelo pings around Provence, in one part of the novel alone, in the rest with Pauline. Blinding sunlight alternates with inky darness. Clearly aware of the need for variety amid the essential monotony of an epidemic, Giono moves the action regularly between houses, villages, towns, open countryside. In the Giuseppe section, the town is transferred to the countryside: bourgeois interiors reappear *al fresco.* There are pairings, mirrorings: two contrasting kinds of nun (selfless / greedy); variant doctors; different modes of imprisonment, and of escape. *Le Hussard sur le toit* is in the picaresque tradition, except that it has an illegimately noble hero, not a low-lifer.

That musical analogy would imply that Giono structures his novel carefully. The opening would appear to support this view, if not the rest. In the opening pages, Giono strives for a simultaneist presentation, panning in stages across various parts of Provence and introducing the first inroads of the cholera. This technique is not just a re-use of that exploited by Jules Romains, John Dos Passos or the cinema, but an old yearning felt by many writers to match music or painting (Bach's fugues, Breughel's canvases) in their capacity for coexisting, cross-threading ensembles. (In *Le Poids du ciel,* Giono had attempted to span a whole night across the entire globe). Giono wished to create a setting, to indicate the wide scope of the epidemic from its first instance. In the event, the simultaneism is clumsy, and hardly gets beyond the level of 'Meanwhile, back at the ranch...'

After this opening, the whole narrative homes in on, accompanies Angelo solely, though it obviously makes much room for his numerous encounters with others. He is involved in all that happens, if only as a reacting spectator or listener. The reader is in direct communication with the protagonist: the lines are open. Or are they? Giono always associated analysis with autopsy, and even the autopsies (medical by the naval doctor, poetic by the hermit) are hardly analyses, breakdowns: they are constructs. Because of his cult of autarky, self-containedness (Giono's favourite image is that of Ouroboros, the snake biting its own tail, and thus forming a perfect self-enclosure), Giono's heroines and heroes house a central mystery, never probed by the author. Despite their readiness to talk of themselves, their self-explanations are more like self-assertions. This is true, to a naturally lesser extent, even of the bit part players in the story. These briefly-glimpsed figures are differentiated each from the other by reference often to some distinctive clothing. Clothes maketh the man, and woman. In general, this most expansive of novelists loves feasting on the sly, *en suisse.* Like Pan, Giono is ubiquitous, interfering, yet he ultimately keeps to a respectful distance.

How does Giono get on with Angelo? He clearly wants both to set up a kinship, but also to celebrate his own freedom of manoeuvre. As often in Stendhal's fictions, the narratorial voice teams up with Angelo's activities, for example when he is washing corpses in Manosque. Phrases like 'il est de fait que' or 'il faut [...] convenir que' (**203-204**) suggest that the narrator is twisting our arm, insinuating Angelo into our affections; that a self-evident consensus is at work. In the following passage, however, the relationship is more complex. Is Giono here being paternalistic, chiding, or forestalling the accusation of naivety?

> Accoutumé à obéir sans retenue à sa jeunesse, Angelo ne voyait pas que ces pensées manquaient d'originalité, et même étaient fausses. [...] Il était de ces hommes qui ont vingt-cinq ans pendant cinquante ans. [...] Il voyait toujours la liberté comme les croyants voient la Vierge. (137)

This comes after Angelo's reflexions on how many people settle for little, whereas elite souls seek out challenges, at altitude (136). It is a contrast between moral strenuousness and *ascension sociale*. The passage reminds of Stendhal and his art of winning sceptical audiences over ('mettre les rieurs de son côté').

At other moments, the narrator frankly castigates the hero with adverbs such as 'bêtement' (55), for instance when Angelo overdoes the business of saving face when it is irrelevant: the little French doctor has bought Angelo's horse back, and Angelo vainly claims he had not been thrown. Angelo can of course be too severe on himself, as when he arraigns himself for ignobility in fleeing from Manosque, and forgets his courageous service with that doctor (86). Again like Stendhal, Giono readily lands his young hero in preposterous postures, as when Angelo struggles mightily to squeeze his manly girth through a narrow attic window and gets stuck halfway (175).

Stendhal (unknowingly) acted as a liberating agent, a pick-me-up, for Giono, not as a debilitating influence (from the same source as 'influenza'). In the late Thirties, when Giono needed a renewed direction and a fresh impetus, reading Stendhal helped him to rejuvenate himself. Giono never forgot to admit his gratitude:

> Son style est plein de raccourcis extraordinaires et fait gagner du temps. [...] Et puis il y a la grandiose naïveté de Stendhal. [...] Il admire tout, même quand il dénigre.[12]

The most obvious borrowings (or coincidences) are: like Fabrice del Dongo, Angelo is illegimate (and Julien Sorel wishes he were); he has a passional relationship with a relative (mother / aunt). Both experience exile, and share dreams of chivalric action. Fabrice wears a hussar's uniform at Waterloo. On the other hand, Giono strips Fabrice of his religiosity and recurrent

---

[12] Quoted in M. Chapsal, *Quinze écrivains* (Julliard, 1963), pp. 71-2.

infantilism. He subtracts from Fabrice and Julien the social unpopularity they both endure, while supplying enough opposition to Angelo to keep him constantly on the alert. Both Giono and Stendhal objected to the levelling down which they held to be endemic to democracy, and they favoured a non-democratic liberalism. Giono takes over the all-purpose term of abuse 'épicier' to typify all those who play safe with life. It is ironical that Giono looked to Stendhal and the early nineteenth century for vestigial possibilities for heroism, whereas Stendhal turned from that period to earlier ages for the same purpose, in his *Chroniques italiennes*. Their joint idol Ariosto, in turn, had lifted himself and his figments from the Renaissance to a mythified Middle Ages, in *Orlando furioso*. This heroi-comic poem, like *Don Quixote* later, imagined outsize protagonists in fantastic adventures. Pauline retains a certain warlikeness from Ariosto's Bradamante. Angelo thinks: 'J'ai l'âme folle, je n'y peux rien. Il me faut l'Arioste' (**457**). For myself, I would say that only unconditional Italophiles would accept ungrudgingly the automatic use of 'Italian', in Giono or Stendhal, as a compliment, an unquestionable value or essence.

In the text of *Le Hussard sur le toit*, Angelo's frequent self-interrogations, his powerful need for self-esteem, his desire not to lose face either before others or himself, are all recognisably Stendhalian. Here is one such heroic monologue:

> Quelle figure ferais-je à la guerre? J'ai le courage de charger, mais aurais-je le courage du fossoyeur? Il faut non seulement tuer mais savoir regarder froidement les morts. Sans quoi, l'on est ridicule. Si on est ridicule dans son métier, dans quoi sera-t-on élégant? (**48**)

Giono rations himself to only one of those ironic footnotes Stendhal was fond of, when Angelo doubts the sincerity of the common folk after being nearly torn limb from limb in Manosque: 'C'est un aristocrate, quoique carbonaro, qui parle, et d'ailleurs fort jeune. [Note de l'auteur]' (**129**, n.). Giono, like Stendhal, is more interested in style of action than the practical purposes it might be put to, and compromised by.

The key proverb for Giono is that concerning the Spanish inn, where what you require you have to bring yourself: sublime do-it-yourself. Giono used Stendhal as an aid to vision, and not as a substitute for sight. He had, moreover, some reservations, for example about the lack of physical description in Stendhal's prose, where it is indeed regrettably sparse.[13] Giono's is far more sensuous. Stendhal's well-known preference for style as a transparent varnish (strongly shared by Boris Pasternak) does not translate to Giono's style, which is more like a thick jam.

While it is undeniable that Giono's first go at the Hussar cycle (*Angelo*) was so heavily Stendhalian that it was virtually pastiche, Giono realised this, and published the text only much later, as evidence of his trial run. Giono is no more capable of sticking to a sustained, programmatic takeoff than he is of keeping to the unvarnished truth, or of merely copying everyday reality. His swigging at other men's bottles had its limits. Stendhal acted as a lucky charm against infection by the cholera. He buoyed Giono up when he needed it, geed him up from his till then largely plodding gait, and generally promoted vivacity. What Giono borrowed, he invested handsomely.

---

[13] See J. Carrière, *Jean Giono* (Lyon: La Manufacture, 1985), pp. 148-9.

Chapter Five

The film of the book

There had been a television adaptation on 11 February 1953, with Gérard Philipe and Jeanne Moreau in the starring roles. A film was mooted in 1957-1958, with François Villiers as director (he was later to bring to the screen *L'Eau vive* and *Un Roi sans divertissement*). As for other projects, we can only dream of what Luis Buñuel or Ingmar Bergman, two masters of death on the rampage and of macabre humour, would have made of Giono's novel.

In the autumn of 1995, *Le Hussard sur le toit* was the top box-office hit for three weeks, grossing $11 million before the smart money went on the zany comedy of *Les Anges gardiens*, and staying in the top ten for seven weeks. As did Claude Berri's *Germinal* when released two years before, it had cost more to make (176 million francs) than any previous French film. With it, the director Jean-Paul Rappeneau aimed to outdo Hollywood super-productions and to repeat the commercial bonanza, on both sides of the Atlantic, of his *Cyrano de Bergerac*. The adaptation of the novel, however, posed more serious problems than did a naturally cinegenic dramatic text.

Despite all appearances (his munificent imagery, his fascination with the look of things), Giono was never primarily a visual writer, like, for example, Zola, who translates so very well to the screen. As a result, the various films based on his works have generally, perhaps inevitably, lacked a vital dimension. Giono himself was very unhappy with prewar adaptations by Marcel Pagnol (*Jofroi, Angèle, Regain, La Femme du boulanger*), and even took him to court over copyright questions. Giono was always more drawn to what could be thought to lie beyond the merely visible, to what had to be imagined or, more often, invented. In *Le Hussard sur le toit*, the hermit's conjured-up inner world is one of hidden depths, never the strong point of the silver screen. If, then, we can be perplexed by the directorial choice that eliminates the feisty nun, a role crying out for Josiane Balasko's characteristic mugging, we are less surprised to find that the doctor persona and his lengthy disquisitions, flamboyant as these are, are totally ousted from the film version. Clearly they were deemed inappropriate to a costume drama, a tale of high adventure and romantic love set amid ravishing landscapes. In the novel, these erstwhile gorgeous panoramas become under the impact of the epidemic preternaturally ugly, diseased, indeed denatured. The film largely preserves their good looks: vivacious colours, the lustrous green of trees and fields and the flawless azure of the sky, even though betraying the novel, make the point, in their own way, that the hideous cholera is an alien invader. Locations ranged over ten *départements*. Giono himself was carefree about transposing or amalgamating various locales. As he freely and smilingly admitted, literary pilgrims would be unable to follow Angelo's itinerary on a map or on the ground (IV, 1338). Topography was ever malleable, even *fantaisiste*, in Giono's hands: a London address in his notebooks reads 'EW7' (IV, 1569).

Rappeneau introjects into the story line Austrian plots of 1832 against Angelo, so as to motivate his flight from Italy to Provence. The film in fact begins with violent confrontation and hair's-breadth escapes. Thereafter, little reference is made to where Angelo has come from, or why at the end, he feels such an imperious urge to return there. In the headlong onward careering, Rappeneau avoids flashbacks, and thus robs Angelo of motivation, goals, and some depth. Though the film hardly suggests this, Angelo's loyalties are split between Pauline and the revolution in Italy. One major bridge between the two centres of his life, his mother, is conspicuous by her absence: her long letter is omitted. Some cinematic exploitation of its contents would have helped to underline the crucial Stendhalian aspects of Angelo's character, his partly introverted, partly extroverted sense of honour, and, of course, his energetic continuance of family traits plus above all, the passionate nature of the son-mother relationship. A film can, naturally, be intertextual, like a book, but not so easily when the intertext is a whole body of literature (Stendhal, Ariosto, but also Camus and other writers of plague fictions), rather than pre-existing films. A letter inserted by the director, on the other hand—from Angelo to Pauline after their parting—gives the film a more conventionally optimistic ending than the novel does. He also introduces at the finale the much older husband of Pauline, who, though his wife often talks about him, never appears in the novel in person; it is a non-speaking part, but as he gallops up on horseback his craggy, leonine features create a striking visual impression. He is politically a legitimist (*supra*, p. 19), as revolutionary a posture for that epoch as Angelo's *carbonaro* option. The conjunction of husband and wife in the film tends to make Pauline appear rather more duplicitous than Giono ever intended her to appear.

While the film provides terrifying Hitchcockian birds and a reassuring, faithful cat to match the literary text, and copes successfully with depicting the physical onslaught of cholera on its victims, the characterisation, and to some extent the performances, leave something to be devoutly desired. The almost novice actor Olivier Martinez captures well enough the chunky side of Angelo, his gamut of physical prowesses, but is not given much of a chance to hint at the more reflective aspects of the hero. On the other hand Juliette Binoche, a darling who can do no wrong for many, appears too icy, even at times schoolmarmish, to justify either Angelo's devotion to her or indeed her heroine status in her own right. On her own ground, however, to which she admits Angelo, there is a telling opposition between his rumpled filth, after his hand-to-mouth existence on the roofs, and her serene reception, holding a large candelabra to fight back the darkness outside her room before later flooding it with candlelight, and here she looks suitably magnetic in her courageous composure.

In cameo roles, old and younger faithfuls such as Jean Yanne and the omnipresent Gérard Depardieu turn in professional performances as, respectively, a pedlar and born survivor, and a police superintendent. As in the novel, the pedlar encounters Pauline and Angelo on a deserted plateau and haggles comically over his horse-doctor elixirs; his role is then expanded to include guiding them to Montjay and being deputed to guard their belongings when they intrude on a social gathering in a mansion (an episode invented for the film). The heroic couple, who have lived rough for some time, upset the genteel, upper-class rituals of the elegant dinner table. Though cautiously greeted as equals, as soon as they reveal the horrors they have waded through, the guests vamoose with cries of panic—all except for the mayor (Pierre Arditi), who turns out to be an ardent admirer of Pauline. The young pair emerge from the house just in time to yank the pedlar back from making off with their precious saddlebags. Yanne provides expertly one of the few amusing interludes in the film, though the itinerant rogue that he plays is a well-tried type. Depardieu has little to do except bundle together vital dossiers before making good, like Angelo, his escape from the epidemic in Manosque, after a brief exchange on the social chaos it has installed.

I referred earlier to the splendid short, *Le Foulard de Smyrne* (1958, dir. François Villiers). Apart from Giono's voice-over, it is a largely silent, dialogueless film. If, as I have argued, the plague in *Le Hussard sur le toit* is tautegorical, self-articulating, this poetic documentary admirably does the job of embodying the cholera as a free agent, a wrecker of normality. We never see any human beings, yet are persuaded to register their absence. Humanity, except for the pedlar who spreads the infection, invisible under his outsize blue umbrella, has seemingly been wiped out.

Béatrice Bonhomme draws a telling analogy between silent films and some key scenes in the novel: pantomimes (not, or not entirely, in the English sense, but dumb shows), and speeded-up sequences, especially of production-line dying.[14] The hell-for-leather pace possible on the wide screen suits perfectly Angelo and Pauline's wilder rides, and his fights with opponents civilian or military. The movie camera is very much at home in the rooftop scenes, with their odd angles and dizzying drops. Life on the roof, with its perspective of clear blue sky, contrasts with grubby, homicidal life at street level. The film shows, as does the novel in this respect, how Angelo is never more free in Manosque than when he is marooned on the tops of buildings. In these scenes the film lets up its usual frantic pace to allow for more meditative moments, though there are many more of these in the novel. On occasion in the text Giono himself exploits the resources of the cinematic double take dramatically, and lengthens one of them, as when he makes an idyllic halt in an oasis of peace slowly swivel into a premeditated ambush and a taut standoff (**408-13**).

---

[14] B. Bonhomme, *La Mort grotesque chez Jean Giono* (Nizet, 1995), p. 26.

Perhaps ineluctably, Rappeneau's film makes Angelo and Pauline *stand out*, from the various landscapes and built-up areas, whereas in the book the couple are each one set of words embedded among multiple other sets; they may, there, be the focus of attention, but they have to fight to keep it. This foregrounding of figures is one of several ways in which westerns spring to mind while watching. When I asked Giono in the 1950s whether he could accept such a comparison (I had in mind the vendetta-based *Le Chant du monde* [1934] as much as *Le Hussard sur le toit*), he acquiesced graciously: he was, with his dog, an avid filmgoer. The common elements are: largely empty landscapes or deserted, sunbaked streets; a solitary hero reading signs to track his way; the self-reliant, pioneering spirit of select individuals undaunted by distance or difficulties; the sudden eruptions of violence; Angelo the fastest swordsman in the South, a lone wolf most at home in the saddle. The area may have supplied some of the locations used in the film, but it is a world away from the dude ranches and touristy *Gardians* of the Camargue. Like the mythical cowboy, Angelo too could warn: 'Don't fence me in'.

Coda

Dylan Thomas intoned: 'Death shall have no dominion.'[15] Yes it shall, but we do not have to kowtow to it, and may die with our boots on. For all the lethal disease, noisome filth, mephitic stink and brutal death agonies, *Le Hussard sur le toit* is strangely, perversely, invigorating. It is as if Giono's gale of words had cleared the pestilential air, just as in *Le Foulard de Smyrne* fire licks clean infected property, when guttering candles lit in prayer have failed to stem the inroads of the cholera. Is the disaster ultimately beneficial, as Artaud argued? No doubt survivors need to think so. Under its chaotic manifestations, the epidemic is, paradoxically, a force of order, one of the brutal ways in which, periodically, a universe conceived, as Giono did conceive it (as homeostatic) restores a necessary balance. Giono, this born writer, this 'bard of Nature', is deeply perverse. He goes against the grain; he finds joy in horror, life in death. He rewrites the script of existence. He is a twister: in the midst of death we are in life.

Happiness is a very rare bird in serious fiction. After slaving over a dying man amid revolting filth, Angelo experiences total bliss:

> Il sentait tout le long de ses membres courir comme le chatouillement de barbelures de plumes et sa cervelle était en duvet frais. (**116**)

This serendipity includes the joys of melancholy:

> Un peu de vague à l'âme est encore ce qu'il y a de meilleur dans les moments critiques, quoi qu'on dise. (**157**)

On the peaks, recrossing the Alps back to his homeland, Italy, Angelo is described, in an attitude and words clearly reminiscent of Stendhal, as being 'au comble du bonheur' (**499**). At the end of *Vie de Henry Brulard,* he had exclaimed: 'Quel parti prendre? Comment peindre le bonheur fou? [...] Ma foi, je

---

[15] D. Thomas, 'And Death shall have no Dominion', in *Collected Poems, 1936-1952.* (Dent, 1972), p. 62.

ne puis continuer, le sujet surpasse le disant.'[16] Stendhal pleads that the state is ineffable; Giono does not even apologise for what may be seen by the reader as an authorial cop-out. Beckett, who had better reason than either to mistrust the capacity of language to express anything properly, at least had the grace to joke about his short measure: 'What has so happily been called the unutterable or ineffable, so that any attempt to utter or eff it is doomed to fail, doomed to fail.'[17]

Angelo's adventures are an outlet for the more strenuous side of Giono's imagination, which was as much haunted by space and free manoeuvres as by cloistral calm and stationary journeys in the mind. Angelo compensates for his unskilled creator: an expert horseman and fencer, but also a committed soldier, which Giono never even wanted to be. Angelo shares Giono's imaginativeness, his sensitivity to sensations, his care for language and, despite the new-fangled 'cynicism', his idealism. The cholera tests Angelo; he puts himself to the test, continuously. He emerges, suitably for a hussar, with flying colours. Is he made more cynical, or less naive, by his experiences? *Le Bonheur fou* will display him up to his neck in other struggles, military and political. In this sequel, the cholera will become, in the quotation Giono borrowed from Mérimée, 'constitutionnel'.[18] By the end of *Le Hussard sur le toit*, Angelo may have learned several lessons, but has he learned *his* lesson? As well as being a new direction, and despite all the differences in style and language, Angelo is in a long line of Giono heroes: non-conformist, impulsive, self-reliant, but ready to devote himself to selected others. Though Panturle in *Regain* plods and slobbers when eating or glimpsing Arsule's naked breasts, and Angelo is fleet and fastidious, they are country cousins. Giono's figments are all braver, stronger, more wilful and yet more selfless, more sensitive and more demanding than, except in our fantasies, most of us.

Cholera, bubonic plague, and many other diseases we thought were vanquished for good, are not dead. As *La Peste* warned at its end, dormant bacilli or viruses wait to erupt

---

[16] *Vie de Henry Brulard*, ed. H. Martineau (Garnier Frères, 1953), p. 414. The final clause is not archaic pastiche, but a quotation from a poem by King François 1er.

[17] S. Beckett, *Watt* (Calder, 1961), p. 61.

[18] P. Mérimée, *Correspondance générale*, ed. M. Parturier (Le Divan, 1946), V, 242.

again and to create havoc in human communities. The epidemic enables Giono to join the literature of extreme situations typical of the 'existentialist' tradition of twentieth-century French literature (Malraux, Sartre, Camus). What more telling way to exalt life than to place it face to face with death? If humans can shake a fist at death, make a fist of resisting it, then the age of heroism is not altogether extinct. Recent film and television adaptations of eighteenth- and nineteenth-century novels speak of a nostalgia for more heroic and romantic ages.

Le Hussard sur le toit helped greatly to re-establish Giono after his 'disgrace' in the War and the vengeful suspicions still harboured against him in the postwar period. In 1947, in a notebook, Giono jotted down a project, *Éloge de la haine* (IV, 1363). For all the pungent criticism of immoral, self-seeking behaviour on the part of most people in *Le Hussard sur le toit*, it is a book born more of love, or tolerance, than of hatred. Though bred, Giono often asserted, from boredom, his later fictions do not themselves breed boredom, or misanthropy. The 'choléra *morbus*' has not produced a morbid book. An alternative title was *La Danse des morts*. It is a *danse macabre*, but ultimately a hymn to life. The latter-day epicure retains much of the earlier glutton. Does anything disgust Giono's imagination? It is all-embracing, catholic (!) This novel offers the exhilarating spectacle of a powerful, amoral imagination in full flight. Giono once confessed:

> Je manque totalement d'esprit critique, mes compositions sont monstrueuses, et c'est le monstrueux qui m'attire. Pourquoi ne pas lâcher la bride et faire *de nécessité vertu*. (IV, 1311; Giono's emphasis).

He knew very well what he wanted to do with this novel and, after finishing it, what he had done with it: 'un monstrueux roman picaresque, cocasse, tendre, ébouriffant et finalement grave' (IV, 1140, n. 2).

Like many a writer, he was hostile to reductive enterprises, pigeonholing. He once spoke of an urge to compose 'un roman qui ne signifie rien'. He undoubtedly meant: a novel that did not mean one single thing. The plague is not a Christian one: there are no original sin, and no divine punishment. If it is an 'act of God', it is so in the insurance company sense: accidental.

Despite Giono's passion for the thrillers and detective fiction provided by the 'Série noire'—a genre whose *raison d'être* is closure, the solving of enigmas—*Le Hussard sur le toit* remains an essentially open text, which respects the privacy of its protagonists. In addition, as it was intended to be part of a series, it avoids any suggestion of saying the last word on its heroes.

Psychoanalytical readings of Giono have for some years proliferated. They are truly head-shrinking, and fail to tame his exuberant hubris, his chutzpah, that 'plentiful lack of doubt' that Henry James marvelly at sniffily in Zola.[19] In its cocktail of genres and registers, its dancing with death, *Le Hussard sur le toit* is a deeply baroque fiction. Giono, like Tournier, is that rare, virtually extinct creature: a celebratory writer. The familiar complaint from students that so much literature is depressing does not hold water before this tonic of a book. Like his favourite pagan deity, Pan, Giono is everywhere in (his) creation, similarly energising it. He is the patron saint of Pantheists.

[19] H. James, 'Émile Zola (1903)', in *The House of Fiction*, ed. Leon Edel (Rupert Hart-Davis, 1957), p. 226.

Bibliography

Ambiel, J.-P. — *Le Choléra dans 'Le Hussard sur le toit' de Jean Giono*. Thèse de doctorat en médecine, Université de Paris VII, 1988.

Bonhomme, B. — *La Mort grotesque chez Jean Giono*. Nizet, 1995.

Brown, L. — 'Allégresse cholérique: angélisme et choléra dans *Le Hussard sur le toit*', *Revue des Lettres Modernes*, «Jean Giono 6» (1995), 107-135.

Bulletin de l'Association des Amis de Jean Giono, 6 (1975). Whole issue on *Le Hussard sur le toit*.

Carrière, J. — *Jean Giono*. Lyon: La Manufacture, 1985.

Chabot, J. — *L'Humeur belle*. Publications de l'Université de Provence, 1992.

Citron, P. — *Jean Giono, 1895-1970*. Seuil, 1990.

Clayton, A. — 'Giono et l'attirance de l'abîme', *Revue des Lettres Modernes*, «Jean Giono 2» (1976), 57-98.

Jacob-Champeaux, M. — *'Le Hussard sur le toit' de Jean Giono*. Nathan, 1992.

Laurichesse, J.-Y. — *Giono et Stendhal*. Publications de l'Université de Provence, 1994.

Maucuer, M. — *'Le Hussard sur le toit': Giono*. Hatier, 1995.

Neveux, M. — 'Une théorie du choléra', *Revue des Lettres Modernes*, «Jean Giono 2» (1976), 99-109.

Redfern, W.D. — *The Private World of Jean Giono*. Oxford: Blackwell, 1967.

Poirot-Delpech, B. & Silvester, H. — *'Le Hussard': autour du film de Jean-Paul Rappeneau*. Le Chêne, 1995.

Film credits

Le Hussard sur le toit (1995)

Production:	Hachette Première et Cie; France 2 Cinéma; Canal +; Centre Européen Cinématographique Rhône-Alpes
Director:	Jean-Paul Rappeneau
Assistant Director:	Frédéric Auburtin
Screenplay:	Jean-Paul Rappeneau; Jean-Claude Carrière; Nina Companeez
Artistic Director:	Ezio Frigerio
Editor:	Noëlle Boisson
Executive Producer:	Bernard Bouix
Producer:	René Cleitman
Photography:	Thierry Arbogast (César award, 1996)
Set Decorators:	Jacques Rouxel; Christian Marti
Costumes:	Franca Squarciapino
Sound:	Pierre Gamet; Jean Goudier; Dominique Hennequin (César award, 1996)
Music:	Jean-Claude Petit

Angelo Pardi	Olivier Martinez
Young Doctor	François Cluzet
Police Chief	Gérard Depardieu
Pedlar	Jean Yanne
Giuseppe	Carlo Cecchi
André Peyrolle, mayor of Montjay	Pierre Arditi
Maggionari	Claudio Amendola
Laurent de Théus	Paul Freeman
Pauline de Théus	Juliette Binoche
Governess	Isabelle Carré
Madame Peyrolle	Christiane Cohendy

Locations:	Aix-en-Provence; Avignon; Beaucaire; Besançon; Briançon; Buis-les-Baronnies; Cucuron; Forcalquier; Sisteron; Tarascon.

Running Time: 130 mins.

Availability: Artificial Eye, ART 128. With English subtitles.